The United States, Israel & Islam

The United States, Israel & Islam

By Jimmy Swaggart

Jimmy Swaggart Ministries
P.O. Box 262550
Baton Rouge, Louisiana 70826-2550
www.jsm.org
E-mail: info@jsm.org
(225) 768-8300

ISBN 987-1-934655-38-2

09-079 • COPYRIGHT © 2007 **World Evangelism Press**®
P.O. Box 262550 • Baton Rouge, Louisiana 70826-2550
All rights reserved. Printed and bound in U.S.A.
No part of this publication may be reproduced in any form or by any means
without the publisher's prior written permission.

TABLE OF CONTENTS

INTRODUCTION vii

1. WHAT IS THE RELATIONSHIP OF ISLAM
   TO THE BIBLE? 1

2. RELIGION 10

3. THE CONTRIBUTION OF ISLAM
   TO THE WORLD 24

4. WHAT SHOULD THE U.S. DO
   ABOUT ISLAM? 31

5. THE UNITED STATES AND IRAQ 35

6. THE U.S.A. AND ISRAEL 43

7. EPILOGUE 66

INTRODUCTION

Just this morning listening to the news, I heard an interesting exchange between a retired General, and the news commentator over a particular Television Network. They were discussing Iraq and the many problems that are facing our nation.

One mentioned the *"civil war"* taking place in Iraq and, of course, he was speaking of the conflict between the Sunnis and the Shiites. The General proclaimed in his statement that while the problem was severe, in due time the difficulty could be solved. The news pundant seemed to agree.

They did not seem to realize that this *"problem"* as they referred to the situation, has been going on for some 1,400 years. They do not understand that the problem is caused by religion. That's the reason it has not been solved before now, and the reason it will not be solved.

THE TRUTH

The truth is, even as we will address in this short Volume, the United States has based the entirety of its policy concerning Iraq, and terrorism in general, on a lie. When one begins wrong, and continues in that wrong direction, the end cannot be right.

We do not understand that it is a religion, the religion of Islam that is causing basically all the terrorism in the world. It is not a mere ideology, not the matter of a great religion being hijacked by a few fanatics, which we will address more fully in this Volume.

Some argue that there was no problem between the Sunnis and the Shiites in Iraq when Saddam Hussein ruled. That is correct. So what was his secret?

It is very simple. While Saddam Hussein was a Sunni, still, if there was any type of insurrection in his country, irrespective as to how it started, and irrespective as to who was at fault, he put it down immediately, and did so in the most barbaric fashion, slaughtering the innocent along with the guilty, even slaughtering little children. He played no favorites.

viii *The United States, Israel & Islam*

We cannot do that, and neither should we do that. In fact, such action, which characterizes the religion of Islam, characterizes the great difference, among many, between Biblical Christianity and Islam. One is based on love while the other is based on murder.

I will admit that we in Biblical Christianity at times are very poor examples of the Love of God; however, I will quickly state that the religion of Islam carries out the profession of murder with great zeal.

In this Volume, we have stated what we believe to be Truth, and I speak of the religion of Islam and its aims, without going into great detail. There are many other books on the same subject that better fit such a role. And yet, I haven't seen many books on this subject that seem to address the problem of the religion of Islam, which, of course, is the Koran, which is the guide of that religion. I suppose the reason is, it is not *"politically correct"* to make such statements. The truth is the truth, however, whether it is politically correct or not. Let me say it again:

Building a policy on a lie, which is what we are doing in this nation, will only guarantee that the treasure is spent and the blood is spilled basically for nothing.

THE PRICE

In a recent Youth/young adult Camp conducted at Family Worship Center, in one of the morning services, a young lady was called to the phone. There she heard the terrible news from her parents that her brother had just been killed in Iraq.

America has had to spill much blood since its inception as a nation in the cause of freedom. We honor our servicemen and servicewomen, wherever they are, and whoever they might be. They do a magnificent job! But they shouldn't be called upon to fight and die for a policy based on a lie. It's a price they should not have to pay.

A STRIKING SCENARIO

In WWII there were thousands of Germans who were members of the Nazi party, who were not murderers. But yet, being a member of such a party, they were a part of the most murderous regime to date the world ever knew. Tens of millions of Muslims fall into the same category.

Considering our present policy, what if President Roosevelt

Introduction **ix**

in WWII had prominent Nazis stand beside him at particular functions?! Had such a ridiculous thing happened, Nazism would still be in power in Germany and parts of Europe. How much different is that than President Bush presently having prominent Muslims stand beside him at particular functions, and then later finding out that these particular Muslims are engaging in terrorism? But the problem is, we do not seem to learn. We keep committing the same mistakes over and over.

Most in this nation have it in their minds that we can change the Muslim direction. It must be understood, that one does not change a religion. The goal of Islam is to Islamize the entirety of the world. And please believe me, they have the will to do such, whatever the cost, they just simply, at least as of yet, do not have the way. In fact, the only thing standing between the Muslims and the Islamization of the entirety of the world is the United States of America. They want to take over the world, institute Sharia Law, which would plunge the world once again into the Dark Ages, in fact, a Dark Ages far worse than that of the Middle Ages.

We cannot change Islam. We have to understand this religion, meet it as it is, and take the appropriate steps. Unfortunately, those steps are not yet being taken.

WHAT IS THE RELATIONSHIP OF ISLAM TO THE BIBLE?

CHAPTER ONE

In truth, none!

While the Muslims have misquoted the Bible, falsely interpreted the Bible, misapplied the Bible, and even changed the Bible, the truth is, Islam has absolutely no part in the Word of God. While the Koran contains illustrations from the Bible, generally those illustrations are twisted and perverted. In fact, while many religions have borrowed somewhat from the Bible, the Bible, the oldest Book in the world, has not borrowed from anything.

The Muslims claim that Ishmael is the promised seed, and not Isaac.

The Bible portrays Ishmael as a work of the flesh, and that he, along with his mother Hagar, were driven out of the household of Abraham.

The Scriptures say, and I quote from THE EXPOSITOR'S STUDY BIBLE: *"And the LORD visited Sarah as He had said, and the LORD did unto Sarah as He had spoken* (despite all of Satan's hindrances, Isaac, the progenitor and Type of the Messiah, is born).

"For Sarah conceived, and bore Abraham a son in his old age, at the set time of which God had spoken to him. (Referring back to the past Chapter, if it be objected that this whole occurrence is incredible, because no heathen prince would desire to marry a woman upwards of 90 years of age, or to conceive such a passion for her that to secure her, he would murder her husband — the very fate which Abraham feared for himself — it may be replied that God must have miraculously renewed her youth, so that she became sufficiently youthful in appearance to suitably be desirable. Three times in these first two verses, the clause points to the supernatural character of Isaac's birth.)

"And Abraham called the name of his son that was born unto him, whom Sarah bore to him, Isaac. (The name means *'laughter.'* It speaks of blessing, increase, healing, life, and well-being [Jn. 10:10]. As Isaac was a Type of Christ, it would not be wrong to say that one of the names of Christ is *'laughter.'*)

"And Abraham circumcised his son Isaac being eight days

2 *The United States, Israel & Islam*

old, as God had commanded him (this was a sign of the Covenant that God would ultimately send a Redeemer into this world).

"And Abraham was an hundred years old, when his son Isaac was born unto him (this verse is placed in the Text so that all may know that Isaac's birth was indeed miraculous).

"And Sarah said, God has made me to laugh, so that all who hear will laugh with me. (The mention of Sarah's name some five times thus far in this Chapter is done for purpose and reason; the Holy Spirit is impressing the fact that Sarah was in truth the very mother of this miraculous child. Sarah had once laughed in unbelief; she now laughs in Faith, a laughter incidentally expressing joy, which will never end. It all pointed to Christ. Because of Christ, untold millions have laughed for joy.)

"And she said, who would have said unto Abraham, that Sarah should have given children suck? For I have born him a son in his old age (this is a poem, and could very well have been a song, and probably was).

"And the child grew, and was weaned (the custom in those days was to nurse children for two to three years before they were weaned; however, there is some indication that Isaac was approximately five years old when he was weaned): *and Abraham made a great feast the same day that Isaac was weaned* (at this time, the boy was turned over to his father for training, at which time his education began).

"And Sarah saw the son of Hagar (Ishmael) *the Egyptian, which she had born unto Abraham, mocking.* (The effect of the birth of Isaac, a work of the Spirit was to make manifest the character of Ishmael, a work of the flesh. The end result of the 'mocking' was that Ishmael actually desired to murder Isaac [Gal. 4:29]. Ishmael was probably eighteen to twenty years old at this time, and Isaac was probably about five years old.)

"Wherefore she said unto Abraham, cast out this bondwoman and her son: (Isaac and Ishmael symbolized the new and the old natures in the Believer. Hagar and Sarah typified the two Covenants of works and Grace, of bondage and liberty [Gal., Chpt. 4]. The birth of the new nature demands the expulsion of the old. It is impossible to improve the old nature. How foolish, therefore, appears the doctrine of moral evolution!) *For the son of this bondwoman shall not be heir with my son, even with Isaac.* (Allowed to remain, Ishmael would murder Isaac; allowed to remain, the flesh will murder the Spirit. The Divine way of holiness is to 'put off the old man,' just as Abraham 'put off' Ishmael. Man's way of holiness is to improve the old man, that

is, to improve Ishmael. The effort is both foolish and hopeless.)

"And the thing was very grievous in Abraham's sight because of his son. (It is always a struggle to cast out this element of bondage, that is, salvation by works, of which this is a type. For legalism is dear to the heart. Ishmael was the fruit, and, to Abraham, the fair fruit of his own energy and planning, which God can never accept.)

"And God said unto Abraham, let it not be grievous in your sight because of the lad, and because of your bondwoman; and all that Sarah has said unto you, hearken unto her voice; for in Isaac shall your seed be called. (It is labor lost to seek to make a crooked thing straight. Hence, all efforts after the improvement of nature are utterly futile, so far as God is concerned. The *'flesh'* must go, which typifies the personal ability, strength, and efforts of the Believer. The Faith of the Believer must be entirely in Christ and what Christ has done at the Cross. Then, and then alone, can the Holy Spirit have latitude to work in our lives, bringing forth perpetual victory [Rom. 6:14]. It must ever be understood, *'in Isaac* [in Christ] *shall your seed be called.'*

"And also of the son of the bondwoman will I make a nation, because he is your seed (out of this *'work of the flesh'* ultimately came the religion of Islam, which claims that Ishmael is the promised seed, and not Isaac)" (Gen. 21:1-13).

GOD'S PROMISE CONCERNING ISHMAEL

Some years before, Hagar, the bondwoman, and her son, Ishmael, were cast out of the home of Abraham, actually just before Isaac was born, the Lord said unto Abraham: *"As for Sarai your wife, you shall not call her name Sarai ('my princess,'* referring to the fact that she was Abraham's princess alone), *but Sarah shall her name be* (simply means *'princess;'* the idea is, whereas she was formerly Abraham's princess only, she will now be recognized as a princess generally, and, in fact, in a sense, could be referred to as the *'mother of the Church'*).

"And I will bless her, and give you a son also of her (this is the first time in all of God's dealings with Abraham that He had mentioned the fact that the promised son would be of Sarah): *yes, I will bless her, and she shall be a mother of nations; kings of people shall be of her* (her *'blessing'* spoke of increase, which includes even the Church and, in a sense, the Lord Jesus Christ).

"Then Abraham fell upon his face, and laughed, and said in his heart, shall a child be born unto me who is an hundred

4 *The United States, Israel & Islam*

years old (Abraham's laughter was that of joy [Jn. 8:56]? *and shall Sarah who is ninety years old bear* (Paul said of him: 'He considered not the deadness of Sarah's womb')?" (Rom. 4:19).

"*And Abraham said unto God, O that Ishmael might live before You!* (Abraham asked the Lord that Ishmael might have some place, and not be completely left out.)

"*And God said, Sarah your wife shall bear you a son indeed; and you shall call his name Isaac* (the name Isaac means 'laughter'): *and I will establish My Covenant with him for an Everlasting Covenant, and with his seed after him.* (The Covenant is to be established with Isaac and not Ishmael. This completely shoots down the contention of the Muslims that Ishmael was the chosen one, unless you don't believe the Bible. Through Isaac, the Lord Jesus Christ, the Saviour of mankind, would ultimately come.)

"*And as for Ishmael, I have heard you, behold, I have blessed him, and will make him fruitful, and will multiply him exceedingly* (the Lord would bless Ishmael, but not as it regards the Covenant); *twelve princes shall he beget, and I will make him a great nation* (the blessing here pronounced was not because of Ishmael, but because of Abraham, and Abraham alone).

"*But My Covenant will I establish with Isaac, which Sarah shall bear unto you at this set time in the next year* (so now they knew when the child would be born).

"*And He* (the Lord) *left off talking with him, and God went up from Abraham.* (Communion with the Lord is the most profitable exercise there is)" (Gen. 17:15-22).

THE WORD OF GOD

This, which we have given, concerns the statement given by the Lord as it regards Isaac and Ishmael. Even though we have dealt with it in a spiritual sense, it can be likened to the flesh and the Spirit, even as Paul addressed it in Galatians 4:21-31. But yet, the information given is meant to proclaim what the Word of God says as it regards both Isaac and Ishmael, which completely refutes the claims of Islam. As stated, they claim that the Lord chose Ishmael instead, and not Isaac. This all came from the supposed revelation given to Muhammad in approximately the year 610.

Actually, the Lord foretold, even before the birth of Ishmael as to what type of man he would be. He said: "*And he will be a wild man; his hand will be against every man, and every man's hand against him; and he shall dwell in the presence of all his brethren.* (These predictions describe the Arab people perfectly. They cannot get along with anyone in the world; they cannot even get along among themselves. The descendants of Ishmael dwell in the presence of all his brethren [Israel], but do not subdue them, and, in fact, never will subdue them!)" (Gen. 16:12).

THE LAST DAYS

There are some who claim that the Muslims will play a great part in the activity of the last days, and by the term *"last days"* we're speaking of the beginning of the Great Tribulation. The Scripture says concerning this:

"And he (the Antichrist) *shall confirm the covenant with many for one week* (a week of years — seven years) . . ." (Dan. 9:27).

In effect, the Antichrist will make his debut on the world scene by brokering a peace treaty between Israel and the Palestinians and the Arabs, and, no doubt, other nations of the world as well, and undoubtedly including the U.S.A. The Antichrist will receive instant recognition for his ability to do this, so much so, in fact, that Israel will acclaim him as their long awaited Messiah. In fact, this is what Jesus was talking about when He said concerning this very thing: *"I am come in My Father's Name, and you receive Me not: if another shall come in his own name, him you will receive"* (Jn. 5:43).

As would be obvious, the Muslim Middle East will be tremendously involved in this. In fact, the situation, as it regards Israel and the balance of the Middle East, grows more difficult with each passing day. Iran is claiming, and publicly, that Israel should be wiped off the face of the Earth; so, anyone who can solve this problem will be heralded as a superman. And the Antichrist will solve it, at least for a short time. The moment this seven-year treaty is signed, will signal the beginning of the Great Tribulation referred to by Christ and the Prophets (Mat. 24:21).

The first three and one half years of that time, referred to, as well, as Daniel's seventieth week, while the Judgment of God will begin to be poured out, yet, Israel will fare very well it seems. But then they will be rudely awakened and, in fact, will now face their most horrific time, even worse than the Holocaust of WWII. Concerning this, the Apostle Paul said:

"For when they shall say, peace and safety (refers to Israel, but will as well characterize the world; it pertains to the Antichrist signing the seven-year pact with Israel and other nations

6 *The United States, Israel & Islam*

[Dan. 9:27]); *then sudden destruction comes upon them* (at the mid-point of the seven-year period, the Antichrist will break his pact, actually invading Israel [Rev. 12:1-6]), *as travail upon a woman with child; and they shall not escape"* (I Thess. 5:3).

At the midpoint of that seven-year time frame, referred to as the *"Great Tribulation,"* the Antichrist will show his true colors, and will attack Israel. In fact, Israel will suffer her first military defeat since becoming a Nation in 1948. Actually, were it not for intervention by the Lord, Israel at that particular time would be completely destroyed, but thankfully, the Lord will intervene.

Daniel said, concerning this very time, and I continue to quote from THE EXPOSITOR'S STUDY BIBLE:

"And at the time of the end shall the king of the south (Egypt) *push at him: and the king of the north* (the Antichrist, Syria) *shall come against him like a whirlwind, with chariots, and with horsemen, and with many ships; and he shall enter into the countries, and shall overflow and pass over.* (The phrase, *'And at the time of the end,'* refers to the time of the fulfillment of these Prophecies, which, in fact, is just ahead. It is known that *'the king of the south'* refers to Egypt, because that's who is referred to at the beginning of this Chapter, which spoke of the breakup of the Grecian Empire. As well, *'the king of the north'* proves that the Antichrist will come from the Syrian division of the breakup of the Grecian Empire. So the Antichrist will more than likely be a Syrian Jew.)

"He shall enter also into the glorious land (into Israel), *and many countries shall be overthrown* (those in the Middle East): *but these shall escape out of his hand* (escape out of the hand of the Antichrist), *even Edom and Moab, and the chief of the children of Ammon.* (Edom, Moab, and Ammon comprise modern Jordan. His entering into the *'glorious land'* refers to his invasion of Israel at the midpoint of his seven-year nonaggression pact with them, therefore, breaking his covenant [Dan. 9:27].

"The countries listed comprise modern Jordan, where ancient Petra is located, to which Israel will flee upon the Antichrist *'entering into the Glorious Land'* [Rev. 12:6]).

"He shall stretch forth his hand also upon the countries: and the land of Egypt shall not escape. (*'Egypt'* refers to *'the king of the south'* of Verse 40, as stated.)

"But he shall have power over the treasures of gold and of silver, and over all the precious things of Egypt: and the Libyans and the Ethiopians shall be at his steps. (The *'precious things of Egypt,'* no doubt, refer to the ancient mysteries of Egypt,

What Is The Relationship Of Islam To The Bible? 7

regarding the tombs, the pyramids, etc. He will, no doubt, claim to unlock many of these mysteries; he very well could do so, regarding the supernatural powers given to him, and we continue to speak of the Antichrist, by the powers of darkness.)

"But tidings out of the east and out of the north shall trouble him: therefore he shall go forth with great fury to destroy, and utterly to make away many. (After the Antichrist breaks his covenant with Israel, actually *'entering into the Glorious Land,'* he will be prevented from further destroying her by the *'tidings of the east and out of the north'* that *'shall trouble him.'* No doubt, these will be nations, probably led by Russia [north], Japan, and China [east], forming a union against him, but which will have no success)" (Dan. 11:40-44).

THE MUSLIM WORLD, THE ANTICHRIST, AND ISRAEL

When the Antichrist turns on Israel, actually, and as stated, defeating her, no doubt, the Muslim world will be aiding and abetting the man of sin in all of his efforts. As well, every evidence is, that the entirety of the Middle East, with all of its oil wealth, with the exception of Jordan, will now be in his control. In fact, Daniel 11:43, as previously quoted, in essence tells us this. So, he will have all the money he needs in order to do what he needs to do, which is to take over the entire world. He will not succeed, however, in doing that. The Scripture says:

"And he shall plant the tabernacles of his palace between the seas in the Glorious Holy Mountain; yet he shall come to his end, and none shall help him. (*'And he shall plant the tabernacles of his palace,'* refers to him taking over the newly-built Temple in Jerusalem and stopping the Sacrifices as prophesied in Daniel 8:9-12. This speaks of the time when he will turn on Israel at the midpoint of the Great Tribulation.

"*'Between the seas and the Glorious Holy Mountain,'* refers to the Dead Sea and the Mediterranean Sea. The *'Glorious Holy Mountain'* is Mt. Moriah, where the Temple is located.

"*'Yet he shall come to his end, and none shall help him,'* is tied to the first part of this Verse, which speaks of him desecrating the Temple. This insures his destruction by the Lord, which will take place at the Second Coming)" (Dan. 11:45).

And yet the Muslim world, who will think the Antichrist is their champion, and because he has turned on Israel, will themselves be rudely awakened. The Word of God is clear concerning this.

8 *The United States, Israel & Islam*

THE ANTICHRIST TURNS ON THE MUSLIMS

The Scripture says concerning this: *"And the king* (the Antichrist) *shall do according to his will; and he shall exalt himself, and magnify himself above every god, and shall speak marvelous things against the God of gods, and shall prosper till the indignation be accomplished: for that that is determined shall be done.* (The phrase, 'And the king shall do according to his will,' refers to the Antichrist, who will pretty much have his way until the Second Advent of Christ.)

"'And magnify himself above every god,' actually refers to him deifying himself [II Thess. 2:4]. At this time, and according to Daniel 9:27, he will take over the newly-built Temple in Jerusalem, do away with the Jewish Sacrifices which have not long since begun, and will set up an image of himself [Rev. 13:15].

"'And shall speak marvelous things against the God of gods,' means that he will literally declare war on Christ. His campaign of declaring himself *'god'* will, of necessity, demand that he blaspheme the True God as no one has ever blasphemed.

"'And shall prosper till the indignation be accomplished,' means that much of the world will accept his claims, joining with him in their hatred of the God of the Bible.)

"Neither shall he regard the God of his fathers, nor the desire of women, nor regard any god: for he shall magnify himself above all. (The phrase, 'Neither shall he regard the God of his fathers,' no doubt refers to him being a Jew. He will not regard the God of 'Abraham, Isaac, and Jacob.'

"'Nor the desire of women,' probably refers to him turning against the Catholic Church, and, thereby, the Virgin Mary.

"'Nor regard any god: for he shall magnify himself above all,' refers to all the religions of the world, which will include Islam, all of which will be outlawed, at least where he has control, demanding that worship be centered up on him)" (Dan. 11:36-37).

Now the Muslims will find out, as did the Jews, that the Antichrist has no respect for anyone, and especially their religions, including Islam. While he most definitely will hate the Jews above all, still, he will have, as stated, *"no regard for any god."* The Bible actually tells us what he will honor.

THE STRANGE GOD

The Scripture says: *"But in his estate shall he honor the god of forces; and a god whom his fathers knew not shall he*

What Is The Relationship Of Islam To The Bible? 9

honor with gold, and silver, and with precious stones, and pleasant things. (The phrase, 'And a god whom his fathers knew not shall he honor,' refers to a 'strange god' mentioned in the next verse, who is actually the Fallen Angel who empowered Alexander the Great. He is called 'the Prince of Grecia,' which does not refer to a mortal, but instead a Fallen Angel [Dan. 10:20]. This 'god,' his fathers, Abraham, Isaac, and Jacob did not know.)

"Thus shall he do in the most strong holds with a strange god, whom he shall acknowledge and increase with glory: and he shall cause them to rule over many, and shall divide the land for gain. (The phrase, 'Thus shall he do in the most strong holds,' refers to the great financial centers of the world, which will be characterized by rebuilt Babylon or possibly even newly built Dubai. This 'strange god,' as stated, is a Fallen Angel; therefore, he will probably think he is giving praise and glory to himself, when in reality he is actually honoring this 'Fallen Angel.'

"'And he shall cause them to rule over many,' refers to the many nations he will conquer because of the great power given to him by this Fallen Angel, instigated by Satan)" (Dan. 11:38-39).

RELIGION

CHAPTER TWO

Religion is that which is conceived by man, birthed by man, instituted by man, and carried out by man, in order to reach God, or else to better oneself in some way. Anything of this capacity conceived by man, is unacceptable to God. This means that anything and everything that's not strictly according to the Word of God is unacceptable.

Islam, Buddhism, Hinduism, Confucianism, Shintoism, modern Judaism, Mormonism, Catholicism, etc., all and without exception, come under the heading of religion.

BIBLICAL CHRISTIANITY

Biblical Christianity is not a religion, but rather a relationship, and that with a Man, the Man Christ Jesus. And yet, much of modern Christianity has been divorced from the Bible, meaning that it is perverted and twisted and, therefore, corrupt. It too must come under the heading of religion. Perhaps the simple phrase, *"Jesus Christ and Him Crucified,"* would come closer to explaining Biblical Christianity than anything else. Concerning this, the Apostle Paul said:

"Now the Spirit (Holy Spirit) *speaks expressly* (pointedly), *that in the latter times* (the times in which we now live, the last of the last days, which begin the fulfillment of Endtime Prophecies) *some shall depart from the Faith* (anytime Paul uses the term *'the Faith,'* in short he is referring to the Cross; so, we are told here that some will depart from the Cross as the Means of Salvation and Victory), *giving heed to seducing spirits* (evil spirits, i.e., *'religious spirits,'* making something seem like what it isn't), *and doctrines of devils* (should have been translated, *'Doctrines of Demons'*; the *'seducing spirits'* entice Believers away from the true Faith, causing them to believe *'Doctrines inspired by Demon Spirits'*)" (I Tim. 4:1).

While the words *"religious"* and *"religion"* appear in James 1:26-27, the Greek words originally used would have been better translated *"spiritual,"* and *"spirituality,"* making it read, *"If any man among you seems to be spiritual . . ."* and *"Pure spirituality. . . ."*

THE GREAT WHORE

The Holy Spirit, even as we shall see, takes a very dim view of religion, which, in fact, has been the nemesis of the Lord from the very beginning of time. We see religion at work in the case of Cain and Abel, the offspring of the First Family. The Lord had given instructions as to how communion with Him should be carried out, plus forgiveness of sins. It would be by the means of the slain lamb, offered up in sacrifice, which would be a symbol of the coming Redeemer. Abel offered up his sacrifice accordingly, and was accepted by God.

Conversely, his brother, Cain, refused to offer up that which God demanded, instead, offering up the fruit of his own hands, whatever that may have been. Please understand, Cain did not deny there was a God, and did not deny the need for a sacrifice, but rather that he offer a sacrifice of his own choosing, which God would not accept and, in fact, could not accept (Gen., Chpt. 4). Cain's unacceptable offering was the first evidence of *"religion."*

We know what the Lord thinks of religion, by what He said in the Book of Revelation:

"And there came one of the seven Angels which had the seven Vials, and talked with me (probably is the seventh Angel; however, we actually have no way of truly knowing), *saying unto me, come hither; I will show unto you the judgment of the great whore who sits upon many waters* (the *'great whore'* refers to all the religions of the world that ever have been, which are devised by men as a substitute for *'Jesus Christ and Him Crucified'*; God's Way is Christ and Him Crucified Alone; as well, the *'many waters'* are a symbol for multitudes of people):

"With whom (the great whore, i.e., all type of religions) *the kings of the Earth* (from the very beginning, most nations have been ruled by some type of religion) *have committed fornication* (all religions devised by men, and even the parts of Christianity that have been corrupted, are labeled by the Lord as *'spiritual fornication'* [Rom. 7:1-4]), *and the inhabitants of the Earth have been made drunk with the wine of her fornication* (proclaims the addiction of religion; the doing of religion is the most powerful narcotic there is)*"* (Rev. 17:1-2).

All of this means that all religion is devised either by demon spirits, or men, or a combination of both. In any case, as stated,

12 *The United States, Israel & Islam*

it is unacceptable to God. Religion is Satan's substitute for the reality of Christ.

To describe religion, the Holy Spirit used one of the most base, descriptive phrases (the great whore) that could be used. He did this for purpose.

The simple meaning of the word is that it pertains to a woman who practices promiscuous sexual intercourse for hire. It also means, *"to pursue a faithless, unworthy, or idolatrous desire."*

Used in the spiritual sense, *"it pertains to religious favors offered for a price."* As well, it will stoop to any level, strike any bargain, and go to any length, to attain its devious ends.

THE RELIGION OF ISLAM

I think I can say without fear of contradiction, that the most destructive religion that's ever been birthed in the heart of evil man, is the religion of Islam. In one overwhelming sense of the word, it is very much akin to the religion of Baal worship in Old Testament times. This form of worship majored in human sacrifice, and I think it is overly obvious that the religion of Islam follows suit.

This religion made its debut in A.D. 622. It began with Muhammad of the tribe of Quraysh in Mecca. He claimed to have received a revelation that God (Allah) was *"one"* and that he (Muhammad) was to be Allah's messenger of that truth.

He began this religion by making converts of some of his family members and close friends. Due to opposition, he left Mecca and went to the town of Medina, both in present day Saudi Arabia. This particular episode, his flight from Mecca to Medina, is now viewed as year *"one"* in the Islamic calendar. But actually it was the year 622 A.D.

THE JEWS

In Medina, Muhammad came into contact with a large Jewish community. Evidently his dealings with them resulted in him being influenced in that he adopted some of the Jewish practices. For example, at least at this particular time, he taught that faithful Muslims should pray facing Jerusalem. The Jews did the same thing and, in fact, had been doing the same thing for some 1,500 years. When the Jews rejected the message of Islam, which they did unequivocally, only then did he change his method of praying, by directing prayers toward Mecca.

He also taught his followers to fast on the tenth day of Tishri, the same day as the Jewish fast of Yom Kippur. This was later expanded to include the entire month of Ramadan.

In his so-called revelation, he also demanded that his followers abstain from pork and, as well, that all little Muslim boys be circumcised, which as most know, are standard Jewish practices.

He also claimed to accept the Jewish Prophets of Noah, Abraham, Moses, and David. He also included Adam in this list, as well as the *"Prophet Jesus."* And yet, he strongly rejected the idea of the Deity of Christ. So, it's difficult to understand how that he could claim that Jesus was a great Prophet, while at the same time being a liar, considering how much our Lord affirmed His Personal Deity.

MUHAMMAD

Muhammad claimed that he was personally *"the seal of Prophecy,"* meaning that he was God's final messenger. While he accepted some of the Scriptures of the Old Testament as well as the New Testament, still, he always perverted the Text. At any rate, his *"revelations,"* embodied in the Koran, became the authoritative *"scriptures"* for his faithful followers. These followers were called and are called *"Muslims,"* from the Arabic word *"Islam,"* meaning *"submission"* to the one God.

Due to his acceptance of some of the Jewish practices, he felt surely that the Jews would accept his message of *"one God."* He found to his dismay, that the Jewish Rabbis gave him no credence whatsoever, ridiculing his illiteracy, and especially his confusion of Biblical traditions. But above all, the Jewish people could not even remotely accept a non-Israelite as God's *"seal of Prophecy."*

In a rage because of the rejection of the Jews, he initiated a policy of extermination that resulted in thousands of Jews being massacred, with thousands of others being evicted from their homes and, in fact, from Northern Arabia.

THE ARAB-ISRAELI CONFLICT

To understand the Arab-Israeli conflict, we must try to understand the attitude of Islam toward the Jewish people.

The land that we presently refer to as *"Israel,"* or *"Palestine,"* was conquered and ruled by the Muslims from the Seventh Century to the Twentieth Century.

There was one interruption during this period of time, and

14 *The United States, Israel & Islam*

that was when the *"Christian"* crusaders ruled the land for less than 100 years. Islam presently finds it unacceptable that this land, originally conquered for Allah by his followers, to now be ruled by the Jews, a people who they considered to be inferior and subservient. At least that is the way it is pictured in the Koran.

The Muslims find it impossible to acknowledge the historic reality that the land of Israel, according to the Bible, which they do not consider to be the Word of God, but rather the Koran, belongs to the Jews. This is the real key to understanding the impasse that exists in Israel presently. The Arab countries, predominantly Muslim, refuse to accept a foreign, Jewish presence in a land that is supposed to be, according to them, a part of the *"world of Islam."*

THE MODERN CONTENTION

Regrettably, most people in the world presently, and we speak of those who are not Muslim or Jewish, think that the problem in Israel, as it regards the Palestinians, is that Israel will not allow the Palestinians to have a separate State. And if the evil Jews, or so the world thinks, would only allow these poor Palestinians to have their own land, all the problems would then be solved. Let's look at that a little closer.

THE TRUTH

That which the world erroneously thinks, has absolutely nothing to do with the problem at hand in Israel as it regards the Palestinians. In fact, Israel has tried again and again, to give the Palestinians particular areas they could call their own, the Gaza Strip being an example. In fact, not so long before Yasser Arafat died, Israel agreed to all his demands regarding a separate State with the exception of one. They would not give up Jerusalem, which he demanded as the capital of the new country of Palestine. So, the talks fell apart.

The truth is, the Muslims demand two things. They are:

1. Every Jew in Israel dead; and,
2. The entire land of Israel thereby being Muslim.

They have initiated several wars from the time of the inception of Israel as a State in 1948, with this view in mind. They have lost each one of those wars. And the Reader should keep the following in mind:

Religion **15**

ISRAELI COMPASSION

Even though the Muslims initiated each one of these wars against Israel, with Israel coming out victor in each one, still, the Israeli's allowed the Muslims to remain in the land. Had the scene been reversed, and the Muslims having won any one of these conflicts, as stated, every Jew would have been massacred.

PALESTINIANS?

Actually, there is no such thing as a nationality of people, or even a segment of people that can honestly be referred to as *"Palestinians."* The truth is, all of the so-called Palestinians in Israel presently, are actually Jordanians, Egyptians, Syrians, etc.

The word or name *"Palestinian,"* actually has its roots in the name *"Philistines,"* who inhabited the area presently called Gaza in Old Testament times. To be sure, the modern Palestinians are not descendants of the ancient Philistines.

If it is to be noticed, not a single one of the Arab States in the Middle East will allow any of the Palestinians into their country. In other words, they can not immigrate, forcing them to remain where they are in Israel, as a thorn in Israel's side and, as well, providing occasion for the world to blame Israel, when in reality, the fault is not that of Israel at all.

America has been pouring hundreds of millions of dollars into the Gaza strip, and to the Palestinians in general, over the last several years, all to no avail. In other words, the money seldom gets to the people, but is stolen by the Muslim leaders.

As well, immediately after 9/11 (September 11, 2001), the Palestinians were in the streets rejoicing over our terrible loss, and despite the hundreds and millions squandered on this lost effort. They were quickly told by the Palestinian authorities, whomever that may have been, to stop their rejoicing, because that may cause America to cut off the money flow. Once again, it's not Uncle Sam, but rather Uncle Sap!

JEHOVAH OR ALLAH?

Respecting what has been said, the impetus behind the Muslim determination to destroy Israel cannot be narrowly defined as a family affair, even though both entities are direct descendants of Abraham, or so it is believed by some (Isaac and Ishmael). The conflict is much deeper than that, in fact, even beyond

16 *The United States, Israel & Islam*

the comprehension and understanding of the Muslims themselves. Yes, there is the matter of engendered jealousy over Ishmael being passed over as the recipient of the Abrahamic Covenant, given to the Patriarch by the Lord. That Blessing and the Promise of perpetual ownership of the Land of Israel fell to Isaac and his heirs, which are the Jews.

"And God said, Sarah your wife shall bear you a son indeed; and you shall call his name Isaac: and I will establish My Covenant with him for an Everlasting Covenant, and with his seed after him" (Gen. 17:19).

But as well, Ishmael was also given the promise of becoming *"a great nation"* (Gen. 21:18) — a nation so great *"that it shall not be numbered for multitude"* (Gen. 16:10). That Promise has been faithfully fulfilled by God. Tiny Israel floats in the middle of a sea of Arab nations scattered across a large portion of the globe, but with the greatest concentration in the Middle East.

THE LAND OF ISRAEL

The land area of the State of Israel presently occupied by the Israelis, is only about one tenth of one percent of the entire landmass occupied by the Muslims in the Middle East. Now think about what I've just said.

That means that the Muslims in the Middle East have approximately 1,000 times more land area than the Israelis, and yet, they are demanding this little bit as well!

It all boils down to the Muslims refusing to accept the Bible; therefore, they reject that which was stipulated by the Lord, and concerning this very thing, so long, long ago.

There are basically two differences between God's Covenant with the Jews and His Covenant with the Ishmaelites. Israel was specifically given the land called Palestine or Israel (Gen. 13:14-17; 17:6-8, 19-21; 28:3-4). The paramount difference, however, is discovered in these words, as stated:

"And I will bless them who bless you, and curse him who curses you: and in you shall all families of the Earth be blessed" (Gen. 12:3).

The Promise is further defined in Genesis 22:18: *"And in your seed shall all the nations of the Earth be blessed."* That *"Seed"* of blessing delivered to the Gentile nations through the Jewish people — including Arabs — was and is *"The Messiah, The Lord Jesus Christ,"* which the world of Islam will not recognize.

Paul said: *"Now to Abraham and his seed were the Promises*

Religion **17**

made. He said not, and to seeds, as of many; but as of One, and to your Seed, which is Christ" (Gal. 3:16).

THE SEED

The presence and assigned mission of the Jews were, therefore, uniquely set apart in marked contrast to those described as characteristic of Ishmael's seed and national legacy. The *"Seed"* component in God's program for humanity surpasses every other aspect of history. In addition to being the Saviour of men, Messiah is also the King. When His Kingdom finally arrives, He will establish and enforce stability. Delivery of the One Who could so bless mankind was the exclusive province of Abraham's Seed through Isaac. The Promise is specific. The Abrahamic Covenant provides the following:

• A King for the Throne: *"And kings shall come out of you"* (Gen. 17:6).

• A land for the King: *"And I will give unto you, and to your seed after you, the land wherein you are a stranger, all the land of Canaan"* (Gen. 17:8).

• A people for the King: *"And I will be their God"* (Gen. 17:8).

THE BLESSING ASPECT

It was the *"Blessing"* aspect of the Covenant that developed the animosity in Esau's posterity, because the Blessing fell to Jacob rather than to Esau, who fathered their people. Had the Arabs embraced obediently the Saviour and kingly aspects of the Blessings of the Messiah, history would have taken another course.

These residual resentments became deeply ingrained in the attitudes of the Arabs toward Israel, and those resentments spun off in manifold and discernible ways as the centuries passed. Scripture is replete with accounts of the heirs of Ishmael who warred against Israel while growling their determination to *"come, and let us cut them off from being a Nation; that the name of Israel may be no more in remembrance."*

"For they consulted together with one consent" (Ps. 83:4-5). Their *"one consent"* was the extermination of the Nation of Israel.

However, I must remind all and sundry, that all who have said that, and tried to bring it to pass, have met, and without exception, an untimely end.

Since the days of the Psalmist, Arab determination has not wavered; however, the entrance of the new religion, Islam

18 *The United States, Israel & Islam*

(Seventh Century A.D.) refined and sanctified the rationale. It then became incumbent to subjugate or exterminate Jews *"in God's Name."*

The whole world has witnessed the tirade of the Iranian President, Mahmoud Ahmadinejad, stating, in effect, that *"the Jews should be wiped from the face of the Earth."*

A man name Sheikh As'ad Tamimi, who claims leadership of *"Islamic Jihad Beit Al-Maqudis,"* focused the issue in a statement made several years ago, lauding such behavior, by stating, as it concerned a remark made by the late President Hussein, as that tyrant spoke of unleashing chemical weapons against Israel, *"I hope he is as good as his word,"* Tamini said. *"The killing of Jews will continue — killing, killing in god's name, until they vanish."*

Thus, the *"Allah"* discovered by Muhammad was a very different god from the God found in the Bible. Muhammad's religion, which, in his view, was to replace Judaism and Christianity, would have a new book (the Koran), a new look, and a new center of worship (Mecca), and all brought about by wholesale murder.

JIHAD

The word *"Jihad"* is one of the great words of the Muslim vocabulary. In effect, it is a declaration of war against all and everything that's not Muslim. They claim that to die in Jihad is to be assured a place in Heaven.

THE VIEW OF HEAVEN IN THE KORAN

• Koran 44:51-59 says that large-eyed virgins are awaiting Muslims in Heaven.

• It says the female virgins will have large *"swelling breasts"* (Koran 78:31-35).

• In Heaven the virginity of these women, according to the Koran, will be automatically restored after each encounter (Koran 56:35).

• Men in paradise will recline on couches surrounded by fruit, meats, and beautiful women (Koran 52:16-22).

• The Koran says that Muslim men in Heaven will have a virtual assortment of sex, in other words, whatever is desired (Koran 55:62-77).

• In the Hadith, it is said that men will have the availability of 72 virgins and, in fact, there will also be a free sex market for

both men and women (Hadith Al Hadis Vol. 4, P. 172, No. 34).
• The Koran claims that in Heaven men will enjoy a fountain of wine, which they can enjoy without ever getting drunk (Koran 37:45).
• The Koran also states that those who wish for the pleasure of young boys will find many in paradise (Koran 76:19).

HOLY WAR?

Holy?
• The Koran states that all Muslims must fight until there is no worship but that of Allah (Koran 2:193; 8:39).
• Christians and Jews must be exterminated (Koran 2:193; 9:5, 29-30).
• Those who convert to Christianity or leave the Islamic religion for any reason, must be killed (Koran 4:91).
Muhammad said, *"Whosoever changes his religion, kill him"* (Al-Bukhari 9:57).
• Those who criticize Islam must be killed (Koran 9:12; 45:9).
• Those who cut off the heads of infidels are guaranteed of paradise (Koran 47:4-6).
• By killing, one is following the example of Muhammad who killed as well (Koran 33:21).
• The prophets of Islam are to promote terrorism (Koran 17:59).
• As it regards all of this, symbolically, the modern State of Israel stands as a constant reminder to rabid fundamentalist Muslims of their humiliation before infidels — a condition that can only be remedied through conquest.

RELIGIOUS DOMINANCE

The issue of land in the Middle East, namely Israel, while very important, is not primarily the great question. The great question concerns religious dominance — the lack of which is intolerable to the Muslim who is taught that Allah is all and is to posses all.
An abiding tenet of Islam is that all lands are to be subject to Allah. Therefore, once a territory is taken, it must remain under Muslim domination. If land is lost, holy war (Jihad) becomes necessary. Any concessions or treaties made with enemies under conditions making it impossible to restore dominion by force are observed only until means are available to remedy the situation.
For this reason, as Arab spokesmen have repeatedly avowed,

20 *The United States, Israel & Islam*

any negotiated peace agreement with Israel will only provide a staging area from which to pursue total elimination of the Jewish presence from land claimed to be sacred to Allah. Hence, the negotiations and peace treaties with the Palestinians regarding the Gaza Strip, Jericho, and the West Bank should be looked at accordingly.

In such a perpetual state of conflict, Israelis know all too well that the Western World must learn or live to regret — survival against the Muslim onslaught means having a superior strength and the will to use it.

MUSLIM EVANGELISM

The Muslims, beyond the shadow of a doubt, are bent on possessing this Planet for Allah, either by coercion or persuasion. They do not lack the will to use whatever means necessary, even to the slaughter of millions, only the way. By devious means, they are making great headway around the world.

In France, Islam ranks second only to Catholicism. England has received such a massive influx of Muslims, so many, in fact, that the face of the landscape has literally changed. In 1945, there was one Mosque in England; in 2007, there are over 3,000. In fact, London is the site of the largest Mosque in Western Europe. The story is the same in North America.

The first Mosque in the United States was built in Cedar Rapids, Iowa, in 1934. In 1989, there were approximately 700 Mosques in the United States. Presently (2007) there are well over 2,000.

Muslims lay claim to some 10 million adherents to Islam in North America, drawn mostly from the black population. Actually, these converts to Islam in America call Christianity *"the white man's religion,"* while Islam is called *"the black man's religion."* In 1989, the Muslims boasted that they would soon surpass the Jewish population in this country of 7 million. They have reached their goal.

Some years ago, Dr. Ishmael Faruqui, challenged Muslims to pursue a goal of 50 million to 75 million new American converts to Islam. He said, *"Only from massive conversion can we hope to elect Muslim politicians, appoint Muslim judges, and incorporate Shariah law into the judicial system of America. We must transcend our minority status to make Islam a dominant force in America and the West."*

In the face of this, a point to ponder is the fact that students

Religion **21**

from Islam countries now form the largest group of international students in North American universities and colleges.

THE ULTIMATE STRUGGLE

There is only one answer for this scourge that threatens the entirety of the world, and especially the nation of America. In fact, there's only one answer for the entirety of mankind, and that answer is the Lord Jesus Christ, and what He did for us at the Cross of Calvary.

The ultimate struggle is not territory, nor the subjugation of people by force; it is instead the acceptance or rejection of the Lord Jesus Christ, Who Alone can save.

Muhammad claimed to have a revelation from God. In fact, he did have a revelation, and of that there can be no doubt; however, it was not from God, but rather demon spirits. As a result, he has succeeded only in leading millions deeper into spiritual darkness.

When one looks at the tens of thousands kneeling around the sacred Kaba in Mecca (sacred so-called) surely he is moved with a deep sense of sadness. There is no salvation in that place or in the stone before which they kneel. The only hope of Salvation for the Muslim world and, in fact, for everyone, is to bow at the feet of the Lord Jesus Christ, accepting Him as Saviour and as Lord (Jn. 3:3; 14:6; Rom. 10:8-9, 13).

The Scripture says, and I quote from THE EXPOSITOR'S STUDY BIBLE:

"*And being found in fashion as a man* (denotes Christ in men's eyes), *He humbled Himself* (He was brought low, but willingly), *and became obedient unto death* (does not mean He became obedient to death; He was always the Master of Death; rather, He subjected Himself to death), *even the death of the Cross* (this presents the character of His Death as one of disgrace and degradation, which was necessary for men to be redeemed. This type of death alone would pay the terrible sin debt, and do so in totality.)

"*Wherefore God also has highly exalted Him* (to a place of supreme Majesty; Jesus has always been Creator, but now He is Saviour as well), *and given Him a Name which is above every name* (actually says, 'The Name,' referring to a specific Name and Title; that Name, as Verse 11 proclaims is 'Lord'):

"*That at the Name of Jesus every knee should bow* (in the sphere of the Name, which refers to all it entails; all of this is a result of the Cross, the price paid there, and the Redemption

22 *The United States, Israel & Islam*

consequently afforded), *of things in Heaven, and things in earth, and things under the earth* (all Creation will render homage, whether animate or inanimate);

"And that every tongue should confess that Jesus Christ is Lord (proclaims *'Lord'* as the *'Name'* of Verse 9; it means *'Master'* of all, which again has been made possible by the Cross), *to the Glory of God the Father* (the acknowledgment of the Glory of Christ is the acknowledgment of the Glory of the Father)" (Phil. 2:8-11).

SOME PARTICULARS REGARDING ISLAM

• Jerusalem is the third holiest place in Islam, after Mecca and Medina — both in Saudi Arabia. Tradition has it that the Prophet Muhammad journeyed at night from Mecca to Jerusalem's Al-Aqsa Mosque, and from there ascended to Heaven on a winged horse.

• About 90 percent of all Muslims are Sunis — considered the Orthodox Sect. Of the dissident sects of Islam, the largest and most important are Shiites — fundamentalists, as in Iran. A split came in 680 A.D. over the dreadful manner in which Sunis tortured and killed Shiite leader Caliph Yazid.

• Some 70 sects and offshoots of Islam have arisen because of doctrinal differences, which, in some cases, are irreconcilable.

• Muslims recognize the Torah (first five Books of the Old Testament), the Psalms, and the Gospels of the New Testament; however, they believe that only the Koran preserves the truth as it was given by God. It is, therefore, the only true book.

• The Koran speaks of a line of Prophets, beginning with Adam and ending with Muhammad. Both Jesus and Moses, according to the Muslims, are part of this line, although they vehemently deny the Deity of Christ.

• Muslims vehemently reject the Christian Doctrine of the Trinity as sinful and blasphemous.

• In Islam, there is no separation between the religious and the secular. All Islamic nations ostensibly declare their adherence to that concept.

• The concept of Islamic Law is all-inclusive. It embraces all aspects of human life and endeavor, both private and public, devotional and secular, civil and criminal.

• Jihad, meaning striving or struggle, is a term that has acquired the Islamic connotation of religious or holy war. Today, however, Jihad has developed into a broader context of striving

Religion **23**

for the common well-being of Islam and Muslims, and not necessarily exclusively by military terms.

• The birth rate in Islam is 42 per 1,000, while in the western world it is only 13 per 1,000.

(Some of the information respecting Islam was derived from articles written by Elwood Mcquaid, Editor of *"The Friends of Israel Gospel Ministry"*, and Will Varner, Dean of the Institute of Biblical Studies of that same organization.)

THE CONTRIBUTION OF ISLAM TO THE WORLD

CHAPTER THREE

Before the question of Islam's contribution to the world, it should be noted that the Koran is the guidance for all that is done by the Muslims. The Koran is their guiding light. They derive, as previously stated, their terrorist activities from the Koran. They guide their daily lives and living by the Koran. They guide their business activities by the Koran.

In fact, there is no such thing as a separation of religion and state as it regards Islam and the Koran. Religion and the state are one and the same, all guided, as stated, by the Koran.

So, the question should be asked as to where the Koran has led the world of Islam? Guided by the Koran, what contributions have the Muslims made to the betterment of humanity? I think that's a good question!

THE ROLE OF WOMEN IN THE RELIGION OF ISLAM

Has the Koran bettered the lot of women? What type of place and position do they occupy as it regards this religion?

Off the bat, so to speak, Koran 4:34 states, *"Men are superior to women on account of the qualities with which God has gifted the one above the other."* So, immediately it is known as to what the religion of Islam thinks of women. In fact, women are looked at as mere property, somewhat like a field for men to plow whenever and however they like (Koran 2:223).

Also, the Koran states that men are free to have as many as four wives at a time if they so desire (Koran 4:3).

According to the Koran, men have the right to cohabit with women before marriage (Koran 4:24). And, oh yes, the Koran states that women must hide their faces with a veil, which is obvious to all who observe women in that religion (Koran 33:59). As well, in the religion of Islam, men can have as many females slaves as they so desire, and they may feel free to have sex with them as much as they desire (Koran 4:24).

I think it should be obvious, at least if the Koran is a guide, that women are given little shift in the religion of Islam. As stated, they are no more than property, just objects.

TOLERANCE FOR OTHER RELIGIONS

While Christianity is very evangelistic, or at least it should be, Evangelism is simply the telling of the Story of the Lord Jesus Christ and His Power to save. The idea of exterminating all who are not Christians is alien to the Christian Faith. The Word of God admonishes us to love all people, irrespective of whom they might be, including Muslims (Mat. 5:43; 22:39; Mk. 12:31; Lk. 10:27; Rom. 13:9). In the world of Islam, however, there is really no tolerance for other religions.

Evangelism as it regards the world of Islam is almost all together by force. Koran 2:193 says, *"Fight therefore against them until . . . the only worship be that of Allah."* Of course, friendship with Christians and Jews are not allowed (Koran 5:51).

All religions other than Islam are merely tolerated. The Reader must understand, if Islam had the power to do so, they would kill every non-Believer (those who do not believe in the religion of Islam), or at least make slaves of them. They do not lack the will as it regards this horror, only the way. If they had the power to do so, they would make the world one gigantic blood bath. If we fail to see that, if we fail to understand that, we are only deceiving ourselves.

JEWS AND AFRICANS

The Koran states that Allah will not allow Africans into Heaven (Koran 3:106).

As well, the Koran also states that all Jews are cursed by Allah (Koran 4:46). In fact, Jews are looked at by Muslims as *"subhuman apes"* (Koran 2:65).

Again addressing blacks, Muhammad called blacks *"raisin heads"* (Al Bukhari, Vol. 1, No. 662 and Vol. 9, No. 256).

Our African American friends should take note of this when they claim that Islam is the black man's religion, while Christianity is the white man's religion!

To the contrary, Biblical Christianity looks at the whole human race, irrespective of the nationality, as one. The Scripture says: *"God Who made the world and all things therein* (presents God as the Creator), *seeing that He is Lord of Heaven and Earth* (proclaims Him not only as Creator, but the constant Manager of all that He has created as well), *dwells not in Temples*

26 *The United States, Israel & Islam*

made with hands (He is bigger than that!);

"Neither is worshipped with men's hands (the Second Commandment forbids the making of any graven image of God, or the worship of any type of statue, etc.), *as though He needed anything* (God needs nothing!), *seeing He gives to all life, and breath, and all things* (presents His Creation needing what He provides, which is provided by no other source);

"And has made of one blood all nations of men for to dwell on all the face of the Earth (proclaims all having their origin in Adam), *and has determined the times before appointed, and the bounds of their habitation* (pertains to particular parts of the world, and those who occupy these areas; however, the statement, 'one blood all nations of men,' eliminates any type of racial superiority);"

The Word of God then tells us what man should do. It says:

"That they should seek the Lord (presents the chief end of all God's dealings with men [I Pet. 2:24; II Pet. 3:9; Jn. 3:15-20; Rev. 22:17], *if haply they might feel after Him and find Him* (Paul is appealing to the action of logic and common sense in trying to address these Athenians), *though He be not far from every one of us* (speaks of the Creator being very close to His Creation):

"For in Him we live, and move, and have our being (proclaims God as the Source of all life) . . ." (Acts 17:24-28).

As the Scriptures bear out, all men in the Eyes of God are the same. In fact, the Scripture also says, *"For God so loved the world . . ."* (Jn. 3:16).

And yet, it can be said as well, that the Lord looks at the entirety of the human race as consisting of two classes, those who are redeemed, meaning they have accepted the Lord Jesus Christ as their Saviour and Lord, and those who are unredeemed, meaning they have not accepted Him. With God, as I think it should be overly obvious, there is no racism. As well, there is no preference regarding gender. In other words, the Lord looks at men and women in the same capacity. The Scripture says, and concerning that, and I continue to quote from THE EXPOSITOR'S STUDY BIBLE:

"For you are all the Children of God by Faith in Christ Jesus. (Every person who is Saved, and every person who has ever been or ever will be Saved, is Saved only by 'Faith in Christ Jesus,' which refers to what He did at the Cross.)

"For as many of you as have been baptized into Christ (refers to the Baptism into His Death at Calvary [Rom. 6:3-6]; the reference is not to Water Baptism) *have put on Christ* (means to

be clothed with Him [Jn. 14:20]).

"There is neither Jew nor Greek, there is neither bond nor free, there is neither male nor female (all have a common life in Christ Jesus): *for you are all one in Christ Jesus.* (This proclaims an end of all class, status, and social distinction. This phrase alone answers all racism.)

"And if you be Christ's, then are you Abraham's seed (Christ is Abraham's Seed, so my union with Christ makes me Abraham's seed as well), *and heirs according to the Promise* (heirs of God, and joint heirs with Jesus Christ [Rom. 8:17])" (Gal. 3:26-29).

The death of Christ on the Cross, which atoned for all sin, lifted the status of women to that of equal with man. Since the Cross, there is no distinction as it regards place and position.

ISLAMIC TERRORISM

On 9/11 (September 11, 2001) our nation tasted Muslim Terrorism. Over 3,000 were killed when the twin towers in New York City were brought down by Muslims flying hijacked airplanes into them, along with the plane that crashed into the Pentagon in Washington, D.C. Many Muslims saw this as a fulfillment of Koran 4:78 where it says, *"Wherever you be, death will overtake you — although you be in lofty towers!"* All over the world this slaughter was celebrated by Muslims and because it was done in obedience to Allah's command to fight nations, which are not worshipping Allah. As stated, the Koran is the guiding light for all Muslims, and to be sure, the Koran advocates Terrorism on a grand scale.

In the Koran, war is described as *"good"* (Koran 2:216). Also, Koran 3:169 states that all who die fighting the infidels will eat with Allah in the highest level of Paradise (Koran 3:169). In fact, this, among other so-called promises, is the means by which suicide bombers are recruited. The Koran states that slaughtering the infidels, and that speaks of all who do not subscribe to Islam, will gain one great rewards in the next life (Koran 8:67).

Muhammad proclaimed himself an apostle of mass murder. Some 800 Jews in a particular conflict had surrendered to him. He tied their hands behind their backs, and then cut their heads off, even after they had surrendered and were defenseless. He then went and had trenches dug, which was at the market place in Medina, and then threw the heads of the Jews into these trenches.

28 *The United States, Israel & Islam*

These individuals were not killed in battle, but were slaughtered while they were unarmed and had unconditionally surrendered. They were slaughtered in cold blood in order to gain their booty. So, that should give us an understanding of what and who the founder of Islam was. To be sure, many of his followers function in the same capacity.

Also it is a known fact, that those who are Muslims, and then convert to another religion, must be killed (Koran 4:91). In fact, Muhammad said, *"Whosoever changes his religion, kill him"* (Al-Bukhari 9:57).

Most of us have seen over Television Muslims cutting off the heads of their victims. This is done because it is claimed by the Koran that cutting off the heads of infidels assures one of Paradise (Koran 47:4-6).

Koran 17:59 tells its prophets to spread terrorism.

Once again, all of this comes from the Koran.

When President Bush stated before the whole world shortly after 9/11, that the Koran was a book of love and peace, the statement was not only 180 degrees wrong, to be frank, it was an abomination. When our President in London was asked the question, *"Do Muslims and Christians pray to the same God?"* and our President answered *"yes,"* again, he could not have been more wrong.

The name *"Allah"* came from one of the Babylonian deities, so-called, chosen by Muhammad. It has no relationship to the God of the Bible. And let all understand, that this *"Allah"* is actually a demon spirit, and when Muslims pray to this so-called god, they are actually praying to a demon spirit.

It may have been politically expedient for our President to say such a thing, but politically expedient or not, the truth is the truth and a lie is a lie! And building our policy on a lie can never come out to a good end. We must ever understand that.

CONTRIBUTIONS?

The truth is, the religion of Islam has contributed absolutely nothing beneficial for mankind — absolutely nothing! In fact, it has contributed, as we have stated, slavery, terrorism, inequality, ignorance, superstition, murder and mayhem. If such could be called contribution, that is their contribution.

There is not a University worthy of note in the Muslim world. If they want a decent education, they must attend a University in the western world. In fact, there are probably more Muslims in our Universities in America, all from Muslim countries, mostly from the Middle East, than any other group of people. We are training them to be doctors, scientists, chemists, biochemists, etc. Regrettably, some, if not many of them, will use their education to try to destroy us. As well, little Muslim children, beginning in preschool, are taught daily to hate Jews and Americans. In fact, this is looked at as a great part of their education.

Most Muslim countries, and despite the influx of hundreds of billions of dollars for the purchase of oil, are little more than economic basket cases.

The following is the per capita income of Muslim countries. The numbers are from 2006 with the exception of the first one, which is 2004.

- Afghanistan: $800
- Bahrain: $25,800
- Iran: $8,700
- Iraq: $2,900
- Jordan: $5,100
- Kuwait: $23,100
- Lebanon: $5,700
- Malaysia: $12,900
- Morocco: $4,600
- Oman: $14,400
- Pakistan: $2,600
- Qatar: $29,800
- Saudi Arabia: $13,600
- Syria: $4,100
- United Arab Emirates: $49,700 (most of the money going into the U.A.E. is for the building of the super city of Dubai. The truth is, the people as a whole are notoriously poor, not sharing at all in the hundreds of billions that are going into the building of this city.
- Yemen: $1,000
- United States: $44,000

In some of these countries, hundreds of billions of dollars are going into their coffers each year from the sale of oil; however, very little of it ever reaches the common people. This means that a handful of people are obscenely rich, while the rest are abjectly poor.

It is the ambition of Islam to conquer the entirety of the world. It's fairly simple to tell what the world then would be like, if such a thing came to pass, by what is taking place in modern Islamic nations. We have heard about the Dark Ages.

30 *The United States, Israel & Islam*

In fact, most Muslim nations are still in the Dark Ages. And if the Muslims succeeded in taking over the entirety of the world, which thankfully they will not, the world would be plunged into a worse time of darkness than it has ever known previously.

Islam has made no contribution whatsoever to the betterment of humanity, and in any capacity.

THE PEOPLE OF AMERICA AND ISLAM

It is strange, but tens of millions of people in the great nation of America, and despite 9/11, do not seem to really see the evil of the religion of Islam. It is passed off as an honorable and great religion, which has been hijacked by a few fanatics. The facts are, nothing could be further from the truth.

Regrettably and sadly, we hide our heads in the sand, and I suppose it's because we do not want to face up to the truth. The Muslim world hates us, referring to America as the *"Great Satan,"* and Israel as the *"little Satan."* Their ambition is to kill every Jew on the face of the Earth, and take over the land of Israel in totality. They see the United States of America as the greatest hindrance to the fulfillment of that ambition.

Our nation is in trouble, and it's because we are leaving the Word of God. And regrettably, the deterioration of the fabric of this country, has to do with the deterioration of the Church. The Scripture plainly says:

"For the time has come that Judgment must begin at the House of God (Judgment always begins with Believers, and pertains to their Faith, whether in the Cross or otherwise; the Cross alone is spared Judgment, for there Jesus was judged in our place)*: if it first begin at us, what shall the end be of them who obey not the Gospel of God?* (If God will Judge His Own, how much more will He judge the unredeemed? The Cross alone stays the Judgment of God. Let that ever be understood.)

"And if the Righteous scarcely be Saved (can be Saved only by trusting Christ and the Cross, and nothing else), *where shall the ungodly and the sinner appear?* (If the great Sacrifice of Christ is rejected and spurned, where does that leave those who do such a thing? There is no hope for their Salvation)*"* (I Pet. 4:17-18).

WHAT SHOULD THE U.S. DO ABOUT ISLAM?

CHAPTER FOUR

What the U.S. should do, and what the U.S. is doing, are two different things all together. America is notorious for not seeing the obvious; heretofore, the Lord has grandly watched over this great nation. But the modern Church has drifted so far from the Biblical model, and as the Church goes, so goes the nation, that, regrettably, anything can happen.

A POLICY BASED ON A LIE

That policy consists of the idea, grossly erroneous I might quickly add, that the religion of Islam is peaceable and righteous, and that it has been hijacked by a few fanatics. Nothing could be further from the Truth. As we have stated elsewhere in this Volume, the religion of Islam is based entirely upon the Koran. To be sure, the Koran advocates terrorism, and even the slaughter of untold millions if necessary to further the cause of this religion. While all Muslims aren't murderers, still, all Muslims belong to a religion that strongly advocates wholesale murder, all in the name of Allah. As well, this wholesale murder includes mostly innocent victims.

We are trying to fight a war in Iraq based on this false policy. We don't seem to understand, that this religion is not peaceable, is not righteous and, in fact, holds to no principles whatsoever, which are very special in our way of thinking. I speak of honor, of honesty, of integrity, of truthfulness, etc. Those things are foreign to the religion of Islam.

THE GREATEST DANGER

America, I believe, is facing a greater danger presently, than it has ever faced in the entirety of its history, greater than the Cold War, greater than Vietnam, etc.

Technologically, it is now possible for an atomic bomb to be constructed, which is no larger than a softball. In other words, it can be easily carried in a suitcase, etc. Such a bomb could

32 *The United States, Israel & Islam*

destroy much of New York City, or much of Washington, D.C., or any other large American city, with literally hundreds of thousands of dead, and hundreds of thousands of others dying. The Muslims hate us. If they can get their hands on such a weapon, and knowing that they have claimed they will use such, we have to take them at their word. September 9, 2001 (9/11) should be a wake-up call! Again, it is the religion of Islam as a whole that is the danger, and not just a few radicals.

All Muslims aren't murderers! However, all Muslims are a part of a wicked system, which operates on the premise of wholesale murder.

In the 1930's and 40's, all Germans who were members of the Nazi party were not murderers; nevertheless, they were a part of the most horrifying, murderous regime, possibly that the world ever knew, at least up to that time. Incidentally, many leading Muslims were a part of the Nazi butchery, because of their hatred for the Jews.

Concerning the efforts made by Muslim terrorists to set off two gasoline bombs in London in June of '07, as well as the effort in Scotland, which was thwarted by the Mercy and Grace of God, many of our news pundants are totally confused that the culprits in these efforts, were not the usual stereotype, but rather Muslim medical doctors.

"How could they do such a thing, considering that they had a good living?" Was the question asked! How could individuals of this nature, some of them extremely intelligent, attempt such a barbaric action?

Once again, these newsmen, operating from the principal of radical Islam, did not and do not understand that it is the religion of Islam that nurtures such murderous action, and not merely a few malcontents.

Will it take an atomic bomb leveling a great part of one of our major cities, with hundreds of thousands of casualties, to wake us up to the Truth?

POLITICAL CORRECTNESS

Colin Powell, the former Secretary of State, angry with me and several others who had told the truth about Islam, made the statement, *"We need more Muslims in this country."* I wonder if our good former Secretary of State has stopped to realize what is presently taking place in Denmark, France, Germany, Great Britain, etc., who opened their doors to the Muslim world?

I'll say it again; our nation is facing a greater danger presently than it has ever faced before. Sadder yet, that danger, which could result in untold numbers of casualties, is being brought on by ignorance, or blindness, or both! As someone has well said, *"there are none so blind, as those who will not see."*

Political correctness, so-called, is killing us. Almost all of the time it refers to a policy that doesn't make sense, and because it is nonsensical.

RADICAL OUTREACH: BUSH CODDLES AMERICAN APOLOGISTS FOR RADICAL ISLAM

The heading is from an article written by Steve Emerson. He said, *"At Wednesday's rededication ceremony of the Saudi-funded Islamic Center of Washington, D.C., President Bush . . . announces latest plan to get the Muslim world to stop hating America: appoint a special envoy to the Organization of the Islamic Conference* (OIC).

"He praised this group by saying, 'we admire and thank those Muslims who have denounced what the Secretary General of the OIC called "radical fringe elements who pretend that they act in the name of Islam."'"

The group our President was praising has stated, *"There's no such thing as Palestinian Terrorism."* As well, they have not at all condemned President Mahmoud Ahmadinejad, who has called for *"the elimination of the Zionist regime."* Also, they have repeatedly backed Iran's nuclear ambitions.

OIC's explanation of the 9/11 attacks is that which *"express the frustration, disappointment, and disillusion, that are festering deep in the Muslim's soul towards the aggressions and discriminations committed by the West."*

These are the people that President Bush is praising. Is it Uncle Sam or Uncle Sap?

WHAT POLICY TOWARDS THE MUSLIMS SHOULD OUR NATION HAVE?

• First of all this huge lie of a few radicals having hijacked the Muslim religion, should be laid to rest. The Truth should be told denoting the fact that it is the religion of Islam, which is the cause of virtually all of the terrorism in the world today.

• We should not allow any more Muslims to immigrate into our country.

34 *The United States, Israel & Islam*

- Muslim students studying in our Colleges and Universities should be sent back to their respected countries. Training scientists, among others, who could later on very well use their knowledge to wreak havoc on this nation is not exactly wise.
- We should know what is going on in the many Mosques in this nation, where most of the plans for terrorism are fomented.
- Muslims who foment terroristic plans against this nation, when found out, should be immediately deported.
- Should we outlaw the Muslim religion? No, that's not our way. However, and, as stated, we should know, and unequivocally so, what the religion of Islam actually is, and conduct ourselves accordingly.

I close this Chapter by once again asking the question, is it going to take the destruction of one of our cities, with hundreds of thousands of casualties, before we finally come to the Truth? Someone has stated, that the only reason this has not yet happened, is because the Muslims, due to the insanity of some of our leaders, are making more headway in this nation by the present means they have adopted.

Also, we must not forget that even those who refer to themselves as *"moderate Muslims,"* are in sympathy with the terrorists. Once again, it is the religion that is the problem!

Muslims do not lack the will in order to carry out their ambition of taking over the world, only the way. If they had their way, and we are a fool if we do not understand this, which means they had the power to back it up, every non-Muslim in the world, would be forced to convert to Islam, or either killed or made slaves. In fact, if the Muslims had their way, the world would be plunged into another Dark Ages of unprecedented proportions. Actually, it is only the might and power of America at this time, and I might quickly add the help of the Lord, that stands between this scourge and total oblivion.

THE UNITED STATES AND IRAQ

CHAPTER FIVE

Up to June of 2007, we were spending approximately 2 billion dollars a week regarding the war in Iraq. Beginning in July of 2007, the amount has increased to 3 billion dollars a week. That's 156 billion dollars a year.

For what?

Beside and above that, at the time of this writing, we have lost over 3,000 service people in combat.

For what?

When President Bush went into Iraq in 2002, 9/11 (September 11, 2001) was still fresh on everyone's mind; consequently, there were not many people in America who were not in sympathy with this invasion.

Saddam Hussein had lobbed missiles into Israel during the Gulf War. If he had weapons of mass destruction, it was definitely believed, that he would use those weapons against Israel. That being the case, we would be quickly dragged into the conflict, so, an invasion of Iraq seemed like the thing to do, especially to conclude and finish what President Bush, Sr. had begun.

It was believed in this country that the Iraqi people would meet our forces with open arms. In fact, that was the case to a certain degree. The one thing, however, we didn't understand, was the religion of Islam. The advocates of that Religion cannot accept anyone, irrespective as to what good they seemingly have done, or whom they might be, who isn't Muslim. Not understanding that religion, we have put ourselves into a quagmire, which threatens to bankrupt this nation, and, as well, to tear it asunder as the result of the loss of so many American lives.

DEMOCRACY AND ISLAM

We keep talking about victory in Iraq. What do we mean by the word *"victory"*?

In our minds, I suppose, it refers to a stable government in Iraq, with the democratic process in place, thereby guaranteeing freedom for the Iraqi people. Once again we come head to head

36 The United States, Israel & Islam

with the religion of Islam.

Islam and democracy cannot co-exist. In effect, such is impossible. Islam is a religious dictatorship, and to be sure, there is no dictatorship, or government of any nature that is worse than a religious government. Such is Islam!

A democracy, that is if it is to be a true democracy, is based on the Bible. While the separation of Church and State most definitely exists and, in fact, should exist, still, the guiding principles of any democracy, and in whatever country, are all based on the Word of God whether understood or not. When the Church and the State are joined, or in this case, the Mosque and the State, democracy ceases to be. Understanding this, there can be no democracy in Iraq. So if we are attempting to put such into place, this is an impossibility.

STABILITY

When asked about what we were attempting to do, or need to do in Iraq, I heard someone the other day make the statement that stability must be the end result. Once again, because of the religion of Islam, such is an impossibility.

This religion guides every aspect of life and living. While there is a form of stability in some Muslim countries, it is stability at the point of a gun. In fact, the Muslims kill each other just as readily as they kill the *"infidels."*

CIVIL WAR

In the last few months, the term *"civil war,"* has cropped up as it regards Iraq. They are talking about the war between the Sunnis and the Shiites. Many of our leaders use the term as if this is something that began a short time ago.

This *"civil war"* between the Sunnis and the Shiites, in this religion of Islam, has been going on for 1,400 years. In fact, this *"civil war"* should be a lesson to us.

Anyone who would explode bombs in the midst of their own people, people who are innocent, people who have done nothing to the opposing side, in effect, murdering them in cold blood, should let us know how barbaric this religion actually is!

Despite this obvious evidence, evidence which is so glaring as to defy description, still, major foundations in America, such as the Ford Foundation, the Rockefeller Foundation, the Tides Foundation, plus others, have donated millions of dollars to

Muslim Organizations, many of them with links to terrorism. How stupid can we be?

The tragedy of all of this is, with the cost of American blood and treasure, we are trying to do something in Iraq that cannot be done, and all because we do not understand this religion. Let us say it again:

The religion of Islam is not peaceable and honorable. It is the very opposite. This means that the idea of a few fanatics having hijacked this religion is facetious indeed! We need to understand that. In fact, we must understand that, that is if we're going to address this scourge as we should.

The religion of Islam being what it is, means that all of the plans instituted and carried out by our government, for all the cost of blood and treasure, will come out to no favorable conclusion. We will not establish a democracy in Iraq! We will not even succeed in bringing a modicum of freedom to its people, not as long as Islam is the religion of that area.

I'm a layman, so I'm not versed in military matters, and will not even begin to recommend anything in that capacity; however, the real problem in Iraq is a spiritual problem, and of that, I feel like I have a voice.

IRAN

Sitting back watching the situation in Iraq and, as stated, the expending of blood and treasure, it is obvious that nothing is changing. Month by month goes by, going into years, and the situation is the same now as it was several years ago, if not worse. So why does the President continue to throw good money after bad, so to speak? Is the following a possibility?

As many have said and rightly so, it is Iran which is the real problem and, in fact, always has been.

Day-by-day the Iranians get closer and closer to the development of an atomic bomb. In conjunction with this, Ahmadinejad and promoted by the Ayatollahs, the real power behind the throne, is continuously threatening the destruction of Israel. We have to take them at their word, and to be frank; we had better take them at their word.

Sometime back, Benjamin Netanyahu, the former Prime Minister of Israel, was asked the question as he was interviewed on a particular Television Program, *"If America fails to act regarding Iran, will Israel take the initiative?"*

The former Prime Minister sat there for a short period of

38 *The United States, Israel & Islam*

time and said nothing. He then said, *"If America doesn't act as it regards Iran, Israel will be forced to do so. We cannot allow the existence of our State to be threatened."*

In fact, the powers that be in Washington would much rather that Israel take the initiative. Israel has been threatened by the Iranians in no uncertain terms, with all the world knowing and hearing these threats. To be sure, these threats become much more serious when one realizes that Iran is on the verge of developing the bomb. Otherwise, the threats would be all but meaningless. But considering the hatred of these Persians for Israel, and considering that they are working feverishly to develop this weapon of mass destruction, it is obvious to all who think sensibly, that something has got to be done. Concerning situations of this nature, the Bible says:

"Because sentence against an evil work is not executed speedily, therefore the heart of the sons of men is fully set in them to do evil" (Eccl. 8:11).

The New Testament says, and concerning something of this very nature:

"For he is the minister of God to you for good. But if you do that which is evil, be afraid; for he bears not the sword in vain: for he is the minister of God, a revenger to execute wrath upon him who does evil" (Rom. 13:4).

This simply means, at least in the instance of which we speak, that at times, rogue nations have to be put down, lest they would take peace from the Earth. At this particular time, the United States has that responsibility; therefore, we must stand with Israel.

This country would much rather that Israel would take the initiative in this matter, that is, if it has to be taken. And sooner or later, it is going to have to be taken.

ISRAEL'S PARTICIPATION

It is known that the facilities in Iran for the development of the atomic bomb, are not in one place, but rather are scattered all over that country. As well, some of those facilities are buried quite deep in the ground; nevertheless, the United States does have the bombs, which can burrow deep in the ground before exploding, called bunker blasters, which can take out these facilities. But if Israel is to perform the task, she has a problem.

Her fighter-bombers do not have the range to go from Israel to Iran and back, without refueling. While they do have the means to refuel in the air, it would be very risky to do so, considering that it would be done over enemy territory. It must be remembered, that Israel's border with the enemy, and in every direction, is only a few miles distance. But yet, it would be very easy for Israel to fly from her country to Iraq, land and refuel, and then carry out the task with weaponry supplied by the U.S. As well, coming back, they could refuel again, without incident or difficulty, thereby solving the problem.

I think the U.S. would much rather the situation be handled in that capacity, than for us to take the initiative. So I ask the question:

Is this at least one of the reasons that President Bush is holding on in Iraq? If we pulled out now, it is a cinch that the Islamic-Iraqi government would not give Israel permission to land in that country, or, in fact, to have anything to do with that country.

So, if the scenario presented does, in fact, have validity, why the delay?

ONCE AGAIN, WRONG THINKING

It is known that there is great unrest in Iran, and especially among the college students, as it regards the leadership of the Ayatollah's and Mahmoud Ahmadinejad. And to be sure, that opposition is considerable. So, there is hope that the government of Ahmadinejad, due to such great unrest, will be overthrown.

As well, sanctions are being placed against Iran, causing great difficulties in the country, even causing a great shortage of gasoline, and despite the fact that Iran is a great producer of oil.

However, the decision-makers in Washington once again fail to understand the religion of Islam. It is highly unlikely that any type of coup in Iran would be successful. As well, it is highly unlikely that sanctions against that country will produce the desired affect. Were the situation what we might refer to as being normal, such thinking might have validity; however, the situation is not normal.

The leaders in Iran have the guns. As well, they are governed strictly by the religion of Islam, which does not function at all in a sensible manner. These leaders in Iran consider what they are doing to be in the will of Allah, and they will pay any price, go to any length, carry out any act, in order to complete their mission, whatever that mission might be, in this case, the destruction of Israel.

WHAT ABOUT DIPLOMACY?

In fact, this is the great argument of the Democrats at the present time. They claim that we should meet with the leaders of Iran, and thereby work out the problems by the means of diplomacy. They deride the Bush Administration for not taking the initiative in this effort.

The truth is, it will do absolutely no good whatsoever to try to solve these problems by the diplomatic route so-called! Once again, it is the religion of Islam.

Even if, miracle of miracles, some type of agreement could be reached, the Koran claims that such is to be used only as a ploy to buy time, that is, if time is needed. Then when the proper time comes, the treaty is to be ignored, with the action carried out, whatever that action might be.

It should be understood, that agreements cannot be formed, at least with any positive lasting effect, with murderers, liars, and thieves. Does anyone honestly think that these people would keep agreements, even if such agreements were made?

Unfortunately, and as previously stated, America has developed our policy regarding our dealings with the Muslims, on a false premise. We refuse to admit that we are dealing with a religion, thereby attempting to conduct ourselves as we have done so throughout the history of our nation. Until we understand, that we are dealing with a religion, and a religion that has vowed our destruction, and thereby conduct ourselves accordingly, our policy will continue to be nonsensical. As bad as communism was, it didn't hold a candle, so to speak, to the situation with Islam. The Muslims will justify any action they carry out, irrespective as to how despicable it is, how barbaric it is, and because they think they are doing such furthering the cause of God. The truth, of course, is the very opposite! But they do not believe that, even as should be overly obvious.

WHAT WOULD IRAN DO IF ISRAEL DID TAKE THE INITIATIVE?

Other than continuing to stir the pot in Iraq, which refers to aiding and abetting the Iraqi's in the killing of Americans, there is very little they could do. While they could send their army into Iraq, that would be foolhardy, considering the weaponry at our disposal. Hopefully, if such an absurd thing would happen, we would have the will to use that which is at our disposal — hopefully.

The United States and Iraq **41**

There is one thing about the kingdom of darkness headed up by Satan that is to the advantage of the Child of God. Oftentimes, Satan opposes himself.

As an example, most of the other Muslim countries in the Middle East are very much opposed to the policy of Iran. They know that the Ayatollah's of Iran consider that the other Muslim countries are far too westernized, which influence must be eliminated. That's one of the reasons, even as I dictate these notes in late July of 2007, that our country is very seriously considering selling Saudi Arabia some 20 billion dollars worth of weaponry. The Saudis are afraid of Iran.

Of course, Israel is very much opposed to this particular sale, which has not been yet passed by Congress, at least as of July 2007. To appease Israel, our government is proposing to make available even more weaponry to that tiny nation. We should remember Saddam Hussein's foray into the tiny country of Kuwait, which sparked the Gulf War.

The Muslim religion has absolutely no regard for honesty, integrity, or anything of that nature. The spirit of this religion is murder, rape, mayhem, thievery, and lying, which they will carry out on their own people, as well as the infidel, so-called. We should keep in mind that that's what we are dealing with.

Considering the overwhelming abundance of evidence, why cannot our leaders see this? Why does the President continue to make ridiculous statements about the proposed integrity of Islam?

DECEPTION

First of all, and as previously stated, this situation with the Muslims, is far more spiritual than it is economical or in the realm of the military. Concerning that, the Scripture says:

"But the natural man receives not the things of the Spirit of God (speaks of the individual who is not Born-Again)*: for they are foolishness unto him* (a lack of understanding)*: neither can he know them* (fallen man cannot understand Spiritual Truths)*, because they are spiritually discerned"* (only the regenerated spirit of man can understand the things of the Spirit)" (I Cor. 2:14).

Second, there is a built-in animosity toward the True God of the Bible, all because of the Fall in the Garden of Eden. As a result, there are untold numbers in America, who see little difference in Christianity and Islam and, in fact, would probably place the religion of Islam above Biblical Christianity. What is

42 *The United States, Israel & Islam*

so clear to Born-Again Believers is not so clear at all to the unredeemed.

Last of all, there is a deception that accompanies the unredeemed state. This deception causes individuals to believe that what is righteous is unrighteous and what is unrighteous is righteous, etc. In other words, the unredeemed, and no matter the degree of their education, do not really see things as they actually are. They are deceived!

To sum up, it is not possible to make a democratic society out of the Islamic State of Iraq, and no matter how much treasure and blood we expend.

OIL

The argument is being made that we cannot afford to allow one of the greatest reserves of oil to be given to the Iranians. And more than likely, if we pulled out, Iran would, in fact, be Johnny-on-the-spot. But we're faced with a dilemma as it regards oil.

We have just spent over a hundred million dollars trying to bring one of the major refineries in Iraq up to speed. By and large, the money was wasted inasmuch as those doing the repairs were not qualified. In other words, they didn't know what they were doing. If I remember correctly, these were Iraqi's who had been given the contract. One cannot help but wonder if they did what they did purposely?

At any rate, even if we spent billions of dollars to build new refineries, or in whatever capacity, to tap one of the largest reserves of oil in the world, how can we protect that investment? There are hundreds of miles of pipelines that can be easily penetrated. While all of this could conceivably be protected, it would probably cost more to do it than would be received from the output.

Once again, Iraq is a Muslim country. We will never be accepted in that country, no matter what we do. As a result, if we stay there five years, or ten years, and even if we double or even triple the number of troops in that country, the outcome is going to be the same irrespective as to what is done. That means that whatever we are seeing presently, is what we will be seeing then. Therefore, unless there is a military reason, as we have mentioned as it concerns Israel, the expenditure of blood and treasure constitutes little more than a waste.

THE U.S.A. AND ISRAEL

CHAPTER SIX

As strange as it may sound, the history of Israel and the U.S.A. go back over 2,500 years. It plays out in the following fashion:

In 586 B.C. Nebuchadnezzar, the Babylonian monarch, laid siege to Jerusalem, took the city, and destroyed the Temple. Judah went into captivity. At that time, the scepter of power fell from the faltering hands of the kings of Judah, and was passed to the Gentile, where it has remained ever since. Jesus referred to it as the *"times of the Gentiles,"* which we will deal with momentarily.

God raised up Israel from the loins of Abraham and the womb of Sarah, for the express purpose of giving the world the Word of God and serving as the womb of the Messiah. They were also intended to evangelize the world. They succeeded with the first two, although with great difficulty, while failing miserably with the third. In fact, in the coming Kingdom Age, they will then evangelize the world, thereby fulfilling what God originally intended for them. The Scripture says:

"And I will set a sign among them, and I will send those who escape of them unto the nations, to Tarshish, Pul, and Lud, who draw the bow, to Tubal, and Javan, to the Isles afar off, who have not heard My fame, neither have seen My glory; and they shall declare My glory among the Gentiles. (The phrase, *'And I will set a sign among them,'* actually pertains to Christ. He will be the sign!

"'And I will send those who escape of them unto the nations' refers to the two-thirds of Jews in Israel who will be killed during the latter half of the Great Tribulation and the Battle of Armageddon, who did not want or desire Christ. The one-third of Israel remaining [Zech. 13:8-9] will then be sent as missionaries to the nations of the world to proclaim Messiah's Glory. They will do so with such success that entire nations will be converted even in *'one day'* [Vs. 8]. Then Israel will finally fulfill her intended purpose to serve as a light to the world)" (Isa. 66:19).

44 *The United States, Israel & Islam*

ISRAEL

Israel was the only Nation in the world, at least during Old Testament Times that was monotheistic, meaning a worshipper of the One True God, i.e., *"Jehovah."* All of the other nations of the world were polytheistic, meaning they worshipped many gods, all in the form of idols. To Israel was given the responsibility of proclaiming the True God to the world, in which, as stated, she miserably failed. As such, Israel had the responsibility of leadership for the world, which was in the Mind of God, but not at all recognized by the world. At any rate, due to sin, that privilege was removed from Israel, and given to the Gentiles. During Bible times, those Gentiles included Babylon (modern Iraq), the Medo-Persians (modern Iran), the Grecian Empire, and then the Romans. The Romans were in power during the time of Christ.

THE TIMES OF THE GENTILES

As stated, those *"times"* began with the Babylonian Empire, over 500 years before Christ. Concerning this, Jesus said, and I quote from THE EXPOSITOR'S STUDY BIBLE:

"And when you shall see Jerusalem compassed with armies (speaks of the invasion by Titus in A.D. 70), *then know that the desolation thereof is near* (speaks of the moment that Titus would begin to surround Jerusalem, which would be the signal that Christians were to leave, which they did!).

"Then let them which are in Judaea flee to the mountains (spoke of all those who believed this Word, which all Christians did); *and let them which are in the midst of it depart out* (means that no part of Judaea would be safe from the Roman armies); *and let not them who are in the countries enter thereinto* (speaks of Christians who lived in surrounding countries, who at this time were not come into Judaea or Jerusalem).

"For these be the days of vengeance (refers to judgment; Israel had rejected Christ; now they must pay), *that all things which were written may be fulfilled* (concerning the fulfillment of these very Words as given by Christ, as well as all Prophecies; to be sure, every single Word of God will come to pass, exactly as predicted).

"But woe unto them who are with child, and to them who give suck, in those days! For there shall be great distress in the land, and wrath upon this people (once again speaks of the terrible days which were to come on Jerusalem, and which did

The U.S.A. And Israel **45**

come in A.D. 70).

"*And they shall fall by the edge of the sword, and shall be led away captive into all nations* (hundreds of thousands of Jews after the carnage of A.D. 70 were sold as slaves all over the world of that day; as well, the Jewish people as a whole were scattered all over the world, fulfilling exactly what Jesus said would happen)*: and Jerusalem shall be trodden down of the Gentiles, until the times of the Gentiles be fulfilled* (has actually proved the case since Jerusalem was destroyed by the Babylonians over 500 years before Christ; in fact, it has continued unto this hour, and will for all practical purposes continue until the Second Coming; then the '*times of the Gentiles will be fulfilled,*' with Israel once again becoming the premier Nation of the world, which they will do under Christ)" (Lk. 21:20-24).

THE UNITED STATES

When the Roman Empire ceased to be in the Sixth Century, it could probably be said that the scepter of power passed from her faltering hands to England, where it remained for nearly 1,500 years. Admittedly, the first several centuries were spent with England gradually getting her sea legs, so to speak. During WWII, this scepter of power passed from England to the United States, where it has remained ever since.

This "*times of the Gentiles*" referring to the United States, is very important, in fact, far more important than the tenure of England, inasmuch as Israel became a Nation in 1948. Even though the sovereignty of Israel is not complete, even unto this hour, at least in the Mind of God, and simply because Israel is not functioning as demanded by the Lord. In fact, she will not be able to do that until after the Second Coming, when she finally accepts Christ. Nevertheless, America's position, at least again in the Mind of God, is extremely important, inasmuch as it is our responsibility to serve as the lord protectorate of Israel. In fact, the protection of Israel is possibly the single most important responsibility we have, that is, designated by God.

This scepter of power is scheduled to pass from the hands of the U.S.A. to that of the Antichrist. This will take place after the Rapture (Resurrection) of the Church. Concerning this, the Apostle Paul said:

"*Let no man deceive you by any means* (in other words, don't listen to that which is Scripturally incorrect)*: for that day shall not come, except there come a falling away first* (should

46 *The United States, Israel & Islam*

have been translated, *'for that day shall not come, except there come a departure first'*; this speaks of the Rapture, which in essence says the Second Coming cannot take place until certain things happen), *and that man of sin be revealed, the son of perdition* (this speaks of the Antichrist, who must come upon the world scene before the Second Coming)" (II Thess. 2:3).

THE ANTICHRIST

In fact, the Antichrist will burst upon the scene in a way that will give him recognition all over the world, and instantly. He will be able to do what the brightest minds in America, were never able to bring about — a viable peace treaty between the Palestinians, the Muslim world, and Israel. In fact, this treaty will last for three and one half years, and will be broken by the Antichrist himself. It was originally scheduled for seven years. Daniel the Prophet foretold of this time. He said:

"*And he* (the Antichrist) *shall confirm the covenant with many for one week* (a week of years — seven): *and in the midst of the week he shall cause the sacrifice and the oblation to cease, and for the overspreading of abominations he shall make it desolate, even until the consummation, and that determined shall be poured upon the desolate.* (The phrase, *'And he shall confirm,'* refers to the Antichrist.

"'*And in the midst of the week*'" refers to three and one half years, at which time the Antichrist will show his true colors and stop the Sacrifices in the newly-built Temple. At that time, he will actually invade Israel with her suffering her first defeat since her formation as a Nation in 1948.

"The phrase, *'Even until the consummation,'* means until the end of the seven-year Great Tribulation.

"'*And that determined shall be poured upon the desolate,'* refers to all the Prophecies being fulfilled regarding the great suffering that Israel will go through the last three and one half years of the Great Tribulation [Mat. 24:21-22])" (Dan. 9:27).

Upon signing this seven-year peace treaty with Israel, and doing, as stated, what no one else had been able to do, the whole world will acclaim the wisdom, ingenuity, and ability of this man. In fact, Israel will claim him as their Messiah. So that tells us that he must be a Jew, inasmuch as they would never accept anyone as their Messiah who was a Gentile.

In some way, upon the signing of this agreement, he will be able to placate the Muslims and the Jews, in fact, guaranteeing

Israel's safety and protection for those seven years and, as well, making it possible for the Jews to build their Temple.

With his ability to bring about this peace treaty, the whole world in a sense will be at his feet. Every Television Station in the world, along with newspapers, periodicals, etc., will declare his ingenuity and statesmanship. As stated, Israel will acclaim him as their Messiah, the one for whom they have long waited.

For about three and one half years things will go well, with Israel, it seems, prospering, despite the fact, that great war clouds are gathering all over the world. Concerning this, the Apostle Paul said:

"*For when they shall say, peace and safety* (refers to Israel, but will, as well, characterize the world; it pertains to the Antichrist signing the seven-year pact with Israel and other nations [Dan. 9:27]); *then sudden destruction comes upon them* (at the mid-point of the seven-year period, the Antichrist will break his pact, actually invading Israel [Rev. 12:1-6]), *as travail upon a woman with child; and they shall not escape.* (The Great Tribulation is definitely coming upon this world [Mat. 24:21])" (I Thess. 5:3).

Considering that the Antichrist will be able to broker this peace treaty, it seems that the U.S.A. will at the time abdicate her responsibility regarding Israel. In other words, Israel's protector will now be the man of sin, as defined by the Apostle Paul (II Thess. 2:3). Now, the scepter of power is in the hands of the Antichrist, where it will remain until the time of the Second Coming.

If it is to be noted, at the present time (2007), the U.S.A. is showing signs of weariness regarding Israel. In fact, at this time, America is the only friend that Israel has in the world. Although there is no indication that America will abdicate her position as Israel's protectorate, and despite the Muslims, still, when the Antichrist comes upon the scene, which he shortly will do so, this nation will gladly pass the baton to him, so to speak, which he will gladly accept.

But in the meantime, the prosperity and blessing of this nation by Almighty God is dependant on many things, but most of all our protection of Israel. We must never forget that.

Why?

• We have been appointed by the Lord for this position for such a time as this. Concerning Israel, the Lord plainly said: "*I will bless them who bless you, and curse him who curses you: and in you shall all families of the Earth be blessed*" (Gen. 12:3). So, our Blessings depend upon our proper protection of Israel.

48 *The United States, Israel & Islam*

* Israel is to be restored as the Priestly Nation of the world, which will take place immediately after the Second Coming (Isa. 11:11-12; 14:1; Jer. 23:3-8).

* Israel is predicted by the Holy Spirit, at least those who are alive at the time of the Second Coming, to accept Christ as their Messiah, and their Saviour and Lord. Concerning this the Scripture says: *"In that day there shall be a fountain opened to the House of David and to the inhabitants of Jerusalem for sin and for uncleanness.* (The phrase, *'In that day'* occurs 18 times from Zech. 9:16 through Zech. 14:21. This shows how precious *'that day'* is to the Messiah's Heart. In that day, His Victory over the enemies of His People will be great, but greater will be His moral Victory over His People themselves.

"The Christian's true triumphs are God's triumphs over him, and God's triumphs over His People are our only victories. Such was Jacob of old, who represented Israel in that coming Glad Day. The conversion of the Apostle Paul illustrates the future conversion of Israel. He hated Jesus, but on the Damascus Road, he looked upon Him Whom he had pierced, mourned, and wept.

"'In that day that day there shall be a fountain opened,' does not mean that it is first opened there, but that Israel will only begin to partake of it *'in that day'* i.e., *'the beginning of the Kingdom Age.'* This fountain was historically opened at Calvary, but will be consciously opened to repentant Jews in the future day of her Repentance. For the fact and function of that fountain only becomes conscious to the awakened sinner.

"A true sense of sin and guilt in relationship to God awakens the sense of the need of cleansing, and so the shed and cleansing Blood of the Lamb of God becomes precious to convicted conscience. As well, the ever-living efficacy of Christ's Atoning Work, with its power to cleanse the conscience and the life, is justly comparable to a fountain and not to a font. The sense of the Hebrew Text is that this Fountain shall be opened and shall remain open.

"'To the House of David and to the inhabitants of Jerusalem for sin and for uncleanness,' portrays the possibility that, of all sinners, the Jerusalem sinners may be accounted the greatest. It was Jerusalem that stoned the Prophets and crucified the Messiah; therefore, great sinners may hope for pardon and cleansing in this Fountain opened for the House of David.

"The entrance of Christ judges sin, unmasks its true character, and arouses a moral consciousness, which approves that judgment. That entrance dominates, adjusts, disciplines, instructs,

The U.S.A. And Israel **49**

and cleanses man's affections, relationships, and desires. All of this must be cleansed, not only in Israel of a future day, but also in any and all who come to Christ. That Fountain is open to all!)" (Zech. 13:1).

Regarding this, the Apostle Paul also said, *"For I would not, Brethren, that you should be ignorant of this mystery* (what has happened to Israel), *lest you should be wise in your own conceits* (the Gentiles were not pulled in because of any merit or righteousness on their part, but strictly because of the Grace of God); *that blindness in part is happened to Israel* (is the 'mystery' of which Paul speaks), *until the fullness of the Gentiles be come in* (refers to the Church; in fact, the Church Age is even now coming to a close).

"And so all Israel shall be Saved (when the Church Age ends, and the Second Coming commences; then Israel will accept Christ and be Saved): *as it is written* (Isa. 27:9; 59:20-21), *There shall come out of Zion the Deliverer* (Jesus Christ will be the Deliverer), *and shall turn away ungodliness from Jacob* (Christ will deliver Israel from the Antichrist, and more importantly will deliver them from their sins):

"For this is My Covenant unto them (a Promise), *when I shall take away their sins* (as stated, it will be done at the Second Coming [Zech. 13:1])" (Rom. 11:25-27).

ISRAEL AND THE LORD JESUS CHRIST

The rejection of the Lord Jesus Christ by Israel, is without a doubt, the very worst thing that was ever done in all of human history.

When they said to Pontius Pilate, *"His Blood be on us, and on our children,"* they have found this fulfilled over and over (Mat. 27:25). And then they stated to Pilate, *"We have no king but Caesar"* (Jn. 19:15). They have also found that through the centuries, Caesar has been a very hard taskmaster.

Even though Jesus met every qualification, in that He fulfilled all the Scriptures concerning the Prophecies about Himself, and even though He would have been the King of Israel had the Davidic dynasty continued, because He was in the direct lineage of David, still, and despite the miracles, they would not accept Him.

Once again, why?

Paul told us. He said, and I continue to quote from THE EXPOSITOR'S STUDY BIBLE:

50 *The United States, Israel & Islam*

"For they being ignorant of God's Righteousness (spells the story not only of ancient Israel, but almost the entirety of the world, and for all time; *'God's Righteousness'* is that which is afforded by Christ, and received by exercising Faith in Him and what He did at the Cross, all on our behalf; Israel's ignorance was willful!), *and going about to establish their own Righteousness* (the case of anyone who attempts to establish Righteousness by any method other than Faith in Christ and the Cross), *have not submitted themselves unto the Righteousness of God* (God's Righteousness is ensconced in Christ and what He did at the Cross)" (Rom. 10:3).

Paul also said: *"But we preach Christ Crucified* (this is the Foundation of the Word of God, and, thereby, of Salvation), *unto the Jews a stumblingblock . . ."* (the Cross was the stumblingblock)" (I Cor. 1:23).

HOW WAS THE CROSS OF CHRIST A STUMBLINGBLOCK TO ISRAEL?

They knew from the Law (Deut. 21:22-23), that if certain types of heinous crimes were committed, that the perpetrator was to be stoned to death, and then spread-eagled on a tree. He was to hang there that day, and then be taken down before dark and buried. All of this was a sign that he was *"accursed of God."*

They reasoned that if Jesus were really the Son of God, i.e., *"their Messiah,"* that God would not allow Him to be crucified, which was tantamount to *"a tree."* So, if He was crucified, this would show to the people that he was *"cursed of God,"* which would say to them that He was not the Messiah.

They figured wrong!

The truth is, the Cross was the destination of Christ, even from before the foundation of the world (I Pet. 1:18-20). As well, the Fifty-third Chapter of Isaiah portrayed the manner in which He would die. It said:

"He was oppressed, and He was afflicted, yet He opened not His Mouth: He is brought as a lamb to the slaughter, and as a sheep before her shearers is dumb, so He opens not His Mouth. (The first phrase refers to all that was done to Him in His humiliation, suffering, and agony. He could so easily have vindicated Himself from every charge; therefore, He self-abased Himself.

*"It seemed like an admission of guilt and, in fact was, but not His guilt, but the guilt of those who were accusing Him, as well the entirety of the world.

The U.S.A. And Israel **51**

"Of all the Levitical Offerings [five total], the *'lamb'* was the animal most used; hence, John the Baptist would say, *'Behold the Lamb of God which takes away the sin of the world')*" (Isa. 53:7).

And then the great Prophet said: *"Yet it pleased the LORD to bruise Him; He has put Him to grief: when You shall make His soul an offering for sin, He shall see His seed, He shall prolong His days, and the pleasure of the LORD shall prosper in His hand.* (The phrase, *'Yet it pleased the LORD to bruise Him,'* refers to the sufferings of Christ, which proceeded from the *'determinate counsel and foreknowledge of God* [Acts 2:23], and which, being permitted by Him, were in some way His doing. It *'pleased Him'* moreover that they should be undergone, for the Father saw with satisfaction the Son's self-sacrifice, and He witnessed with joy man's Redemption and Deliverance affected thereby.

"*'He has put Him to grief,'* actually says, *'He has put Him to sicknesses'* or *'He has made Him sick.'* This spoke of the time He was on the Cross bearing our sins and *'sicknesses'* [Mat. 8:16-17; I Pet. 2:24]. And yet, while all sin and sickness were atoned at the Cross, the total effects of such will not be completely dissipated until the coming Resurrection [Rom. 8:23].

"*'When You shall make His soul an offering for sin,'* is powerful indeed! The word *'offering'* in the Hebrew is *'Asham,'* and means *'Trespass Offering,'* an *'offering for sin.'*

"Offerings for sin, or *'guilt offerings,'* were distinct from *'sin offerings.'* The object of the former was *'satisfaction';* of the latter, *'expiation.'* The Servant of Jehovah was, however, to be both. He was both the *'Sin Offering'* and the *'Guilt Offering.'*

"This completely destroys the idea that Jesus died spiritually on the Cross, meaning that He became a sinner on the Cross, and died and went to Hell as all sinners, and was born again in Hell after three days and nights of suffering, etc. None of that is in the Word of God. While Jesus definitely was a *'in Offering,'* He was not a sinner, and did not become a sinner on the Cross. To have done so would have destroyed His Perfection of Sacrifice, which was demanded by God. In other words, the Sacrifice had to be perfect, and He was Perfect in every respect.

"*'He shall see His seed,'* refers to all His *'true followers,'* which include all who have ever been Born-Again.

"*'He shall prolong His days,'* refers to His Resurrection.

"*'And the pleasure of the LORD shall prosper in His Hand,'* refers to the great victory that He would win at Calvary, which

52 *The United States, Israel & Islam*

will ultimately restore everything that Adam lost)" (Isa. 53:10).

Even though Jesus was put on the Cross, i.e., *"the Tree,"* which was necessary in order that He may atone for all sin, even the most heinous of sins, still, He wasn't cursed by God. In fact, he was *"made a curse."* Paul said:

"Christ has redeemed us from the curse of the Law (He did so on the Cross), *being made a curse for us* (He took the penalty of the Law, which was death)*: for it is written, cursed is everyone who hangs on a tree* [Deut. 21:22-23])" (Gal. 3:13).

Being *"made a curse"* is altogether different than *"being cursed."* Christ had to be *"made a curse,"* simply because He had never sinned. He, therefore, went to the Cross, which was a planned destination, in order to offer up Himself as a Perfect Sacrifice, which alone, would satisfy the demands of a thrice-Holy God.

So, the Jews stumbled at the Cross. They couldn't understand how that He could be crucified on a tree, and at the same time be their Messiah, and thereby the Son of God. They didn't realize that He went to the Cross as a Substitute for sinners, in order to pay the price that we could not pay.

THE RESTORATION OF ISRAEL

The Antichrist at the midpoint of the seven-year treaty he has perfected, will break that treaty, even attacking Israel, thereby showing His true colors. Israel will realize they have been played for the fool.

In fact, Israel will then suffer her first military defeat since becoming a Nation in 1948. At that time, the Nation would be completely destroyed, were it not for the intervention of the Lord. When the Antichrist turns on Israel, this will, no doubt, greatly please the Muslims; however, their joy will be short-lived. He will then turn on them. He will, in fact, do away with all religions, at least where he is in control (Dan. 11:36).

At that time, according to the Prophet Daniel, the Antichrist will hear *"tidings out of the east and out of the north which shall trouble him: therefore he shall go forth with great fury to destroy, and utterly to make away many"* (Dan. 11:44).

In effect, the Antichrist will leave Israel to a later time, in order to consolidate his empire, and further his ambition to take over the entirety of the world. He will not succeed in the latter, but will come close. In fact, he will be stopped by the Second Coming.

During this three and one half year period of time, the latter part of the Great Tribulation spoken of by Christ (Mat. 24:21), Israel will suffer greater than she has suffered in all of her history, even greater than the Holocaust of WWII.

During that last three and one half years of the Great Tribulation, the Antichrist will take every opportunity to kill as many Jews as possible. And then to bring about the *"final solution,"* he will amass possibly the greatest army the world has ever known, all in order to totally annihilate Israel from the face of the Earth. In other words, this will be Satan's trump card. What Haman, Herod, and Hitler could not do, he will do, or so he thinks!

THE BATTLE OF ARMAGEDDON

There is no Biblical indication that the United States will be represented in the Battle of Armageddon. They may very well be; however, there is no indication in Scripture one way or the other.

By the time of this battle, the evidence is that the Antichrist will by this time have defeated Russia, and possibly China and Japan (Dan. 11:44). In fact, there's nothing now that can stop him, or so he thinks. He will take over the entirety of the world. But first, he must exact the final solution. Israel, once and for all, must be destroyed, down to the last man.

WHY WILL HE BE SO DEAD SET ON DESTROYING ISRAEL?

As far as presently being a threat to him, they do not anymore constitute such. The reason is this:

Satan, of course, will heavily persuade the man of sin to take this action against Israel. He will do it for the following reason. In fact, Satan's ambition is far greater than the destruction of Israel. He has in mind the winning of this conflict as it regards light and darkness. He wants to be God! In fact, he has said the following:

"I will ascend into Heaven, I will exalt my throne above the stars of God: I will sit also upon the mount of the congregation, in the sides of the north:

"I will ascend above the heights of the clouds; I will be like the Most High. (In these two verses, we see the foment of Satan's rebellion and revolution against God. It seems that Lucifer, while true to the Lord, was given dominion of the Earth, which was before Adam. After his fall, he worked deceitfully to get other angelic rulers to follow him in his war against God, in

54 *The United States, Israel & Islam*

fact, succeeding with some)" (Isa. 14:13-14).

So, how can Satan, be he ever so powerful, still but a creature, hope to overcome the Creator, Who is all-powerful?

SATAN'S METHOD

The manner in which the Evil One will attempt to dethrone God, is not by pitting strength against strength, of which he would have no chance, but rather, causing the Word of God to fail in some way. If that happens, even to the smallest degree, Satan has won the conflict. Jesus said, and concerning the Word of God:

"For verily I say unto you (proclaims the ultimate authority!), *till Heaven and Earth pass* (means to be changed, or pass from one condition to another, which will take place in the coming Perfect Age [Rev., Chpts. 21-22]), *one jot* (smallest letter in the Hebrew alphabet) *or one tittle* (a minute ornamental finish to ancient Hebrew letters) *shall in no wise pass from the Law, till all be fulfilled"* (Mat. 5:18).

The Holy Spirit said:

"Forever, O LORD, Your Word is settled in Heaven (God's Word is eternal)" (Ps. 119:89).

Possibly one could say without fear of contradiction, that the greatest Promises in the Word of God concern the future restoration and blessing of Israel. More space is dedicated to this one prediction than possibly anything else. So, if Satan can destroy Israel, which he has tried repeatedly to do through the ages, but will now put all of his ambition into this one effort, he will then have defeated God.

THE ARMY OF THE ANTICHRIST

As to exactly how large this army will be, we aren't told. But one thing is certain, it will be many times larger than the small army of Israel. As well, it will have the latest in weaponry. The oil money from the Muslim states will, no doubt, have flowed into his coffers. The Scripture says concerning this:

"But he shall have power over the treasures of gold and of silver" (Dan. 11:43).

There is no evidence that he will have an atomic bomb, or else possibly he does have it, but doesn't want to use it on Israel, intending to make this land a shrine to himself. The radiation from an atomic device would hinder those plans.

The U.S.A. And Israel **55**

Without a doubt, every news agency in the world will be present beaming by Television all over the world, the events of this battle. In fact, the Antichrist will demand this to be done, desiring the whole world to witness the annihilation of these ancient people. As stated, he will do, or so he thinks, what Haman, Herod and Hitler could not do.

THE CRY OF ISRAEL

The Lord spoke through the great Prophet Zechariah: *"For I will gather all nations against Jerusalem to battle; and the city shall be taken, and the houses rifled, and the women ravished; and half of the city shall go forth into captivity, and the residue of the people shall not be cut off from the city.* (The first phrase refers to the mobilization of the nations to Armageddon [Ezek., Chpts. 38-39; Joel, Chpt. 3; Rev. 16:13-16; 19:11-21].

"'*And the city shall be taken,*' actually means that the Antichrist will prepare to take Jerusalem, with actually half of it being taken. The phrase, '*And the houses rifled, and the women ravished,*' expresses extreme cruelty practiced by the army of the Antichrist.

"'*And half of the city shall go forth into captivity,*' means that half of Jerusalem will fall to the advances of the Antichrist, with the other half fighting furiously to save themselves, but with futility, other than the Coming of the Lord. Actually, the phrasing of the sentence structure portrays Israel fighting with a ferocity that knows no bounds, but yet not able to stand against the powerful onslaught of the combined armies of the man of sin.

"'*And the residue of the people shall not be cut off from the city,*' refers to the army of Israel already cut to pieces, but determined to defend the city, even house to house, and, if necessary, to die to the last man)" (Zech. 14:2).

Nearly 2,800 years ago, the great Prophet Isaiah, in essence, prophesied the very words that Israel will say during the Battle of Armageddon, when it looks like they will be destroyed. There will be no nation to help them. It seems that America has bowed out. So, their only hope is the coming of the Messiah.

The following is the gist of what they will say at that time, when it looks like all hope is lost. I quote from THE EXPOSITOR'S STUDY BIBLE:

"But we are all as an unclean thing, and all our righteousnesses are as filthy rags; and we all do fade as a leaf; and

56 *The United States, Israel & Islam*

our iniquities, like the wind, have taken us away. (Here Israel confesses the reason for their desperate condition. At long last, they own up as to exactly what it is, *'our iniquities.'*

"The phrase, *'But we are all as an unclean thing,'* is actually saying before God that they are a spiritual leper. They now recognize that their self-righteousness is no more than *'filthy rags,'* which referred to the menstrual flux of a woman regarding her monthly period.

'It is very difficult for men, and especially religious men, to admit to such! Hence, not many religious men are Saved!)

"*And there is none who calls upon Your name, who stirs up himself to take hold of You: for You have hid Your face from us, and have consumed us, because of our iniquities.* (Once again, Israel admits that it is her *'iniquities'* which have brought about the Judgment of God upon her. She has only herself to blame!)

"*But now, O LORD, You are our Father; we are the clay, and You our potter; and we all are the work of Your Hand.* (In this Passage is the gist of the great Salvation Message of Christianity. Only God can change the shape of the clay, thereby molding the vessel into the shape and design that is desired, thereby mending the flaws and weaknesses.)

"*Be not wroth very sore, O LORD, neither remember iniquity forever: behold, see, we beseech You, we are Your People.* (The appeal here is for God to begin all over again, like the potter with the clay. The idea of the phrase, *'Be not wroth very sore,'* refers to the fact that God had become very angry with His People. The reason for that anger was sin on the part of Israel. God cannot abide sin in the lives of His Own People anymore than He can in the wicked.)

"*Your holy cities are a wilderness, Zion is a wilderness, Jerusalem a desolation.* (As we have stated, the entirety of this prayer of Repentance, which actually began in the Fifteenth Verse of the previous Chapter, will be prayed by Israel at the end of the Great Tribulation, at the Battle of Armageddon.

"*Our holy and our beautiful house, where our fathers praised You, is burned up with fire: and all our pleasant things are laid waste.* (This speaks of the Temple that is yet to be built in Jerusalem. In fact, when the Antichrist turns on Israel, he will make their Temple his religious headquarters, committing every act of vileness that one could think.)

"*Will You refrain Yourself for these things, O LORD? Will You hold Your peace, and afflict us very sore?* (Israel first repents of her terrible sins, pleading God's Mercy, Grace, and Love.

They then bring to His attention the terrible plight of the *'holy cities,'* and of *'Jerusalem.'* Last of all, they proclaim to Him the destruction of the Temple.

"They then ask, *'Will You refrain Yourself for these things, O LORD?'*

"The answer is certain. He will not refrain Himself! He will not hold His peace!)" (Isa. 64:6-12).

THE SECOND COMING

When this prayer of Repentance is prayed, the Scripture then says: *"Then shall the LORD go forth, and fight against those nations, as when He fought in the day of battle.* ('Then' is the key word!)

"1. *'Then':* when Israel will begin to cry to God for Deliverance, knowing that He is their only hope.

"2. *'Then':* when half of Jerusalem has fallen and it looks like the other half is about to fall.

"3. *'Then':* when it looks like every Jew will be annihilated, with two-thirds already killed.

"4. *'Then':* when it looks like the Promises of God made to the Patriarchs and Prophets of old will fall down.

"5. *'Then':* when it looks like the Antichrist will win this conflict, which will make Satan the lord of the Earth.

"The phrase, *'Then, shall the LORD go forth,'* refers to the Second Coming, which will be the most cataclysmic event that the world has ever known.

"*'And fight against those nations,'* pertains to the nations under the banner of the Antichrist, which have set out to destroy Israel, and actually with annihilation in mind.

"*'As when He fought in the day of battle,'* probably refers to the time when the Lord led the Children of Israel out of Egypt by the way of the Red Sea [Ex. 14:14; 15:3]. This was Israel's first battle when Jehovah Messiah *'went forth'* and fought for them. Israel then passed through a valley between mountains of water; in this, their last battle, they will escape through a valley between mountains of rock, which the next verse proclaims)" (Zech. 14:3).

No doubt, the news will be going out all over the world, with most of humanity observing the events in Israel, and particularly in Jerusalem, with the Antichrist announcing victory after victory.

At a given point in time, no doubt, one of the Television newscasters will look up toward the heavens, and will observe

58 *The United States, Israel & Islam*

a sight never before seen in human history. No doubt, he will first attempt to describe what he's seeing, thinking possibly that this is a new weapon brought on by the Antichrist. He, and, no doubt, hundreds of other newsmen, and possibly thousands, will quickly learn, however, that this is different than anything that has ever been.

The very heavens themselves seem to be alive. Lightning is flashing from one corner to the other. In fact, the very heavens themselves seem to be putting on a display. And why not, their Creator is coming back to take possession.

The One leading this vast army, is unlike anyone that's ever been seen. Concerning Him, the Scripture says:

"And I saw Heaven open (records the final Prophetic hour regarding the Second Coming, without a doubt the greatest moment in human history), *and behold a white horse* (in effect, proclaims a war horse [Zech. 14:3]); *and He Who sat upon him was called Faithful and True* (faithful to His Promises and True to His Judgments; He contrasts with the false Messiah of Rev. 6:2, who was neither faithful nor true), *and in Righteousness He does Judge and make war* (refers to the manner of His Second Coming).

"His eyes were as a flame of fire (represents Judgment), *and on His Head were many crowns* (represents the fact that He will not be Lord of just one realm; He will be Lord of all realms); *and He had a Name written, that no man knew, but He Himself* (not meaning that it is unknown, but rather it is definitely unknowable; it will remain unreachable to man, meaning that its depths can never be fully plumbed).

"And He was clothed with a vesture dipped in Blood (speaks of the Cross where He shed His Life's Blood, which gives Him the right to Judge the world): *and His Name is called the Word of God.* (His revealed Name is the Word of God, for He revealed God in His Grace and Power to make Him known, so the Believer can say, *'I know Him.'*)

"And the armies which were in Heaven followed Him upon white horses (these *'armies'* are the Saints of God, in fact, all the Saints who have ever lived, meaning we will be with Him at the Second Coming), *clothed in fine linen, white and clean.* (Harks back to Verse 8. It is the Righteousness of the Saints, all made possible by the Cross.)

"And out of His Mouth goes a sharp sword (represents Christ functioning totally and completely in the realm of the Word of God), *that with it He should smite the nations* (refers to all the

nations that will join the Antichrist in his efforts to destroy Israel; it is the Battle of Armageddon): *and He shall rule them with a rod of iron* (refers to the fact that the Lord of Glory will not allow or tolerate in any shape, form, or fashion that which *'steals, kills, and destroys'*): *and He treads the winepress of the fierceness and wrath of Almighty God* (refers to the Battle of Armageddon).

"And He has on His vesture and on His thigh a name written KING OF KINGS AND LORD OF LORDS* (proclaims the fact that there will be no doubt as to Who He actually is).

"*And I saw an Angel standing in the sun* (proclaims the fact that Faith believes what is written, even if the mind cannot comprehend what is written); *and he cried with a loud voice, saying to all the fowls who fly in the midst of Heaven* (denotes, as is obvious, supremacy over the Creation), *come and gather yourselves together unto the supper of the Great God* (this is symbolic, but it is spoken in this way to proclaim the magnitude of that coming time [Ezek. 39:2, 11-12]);

"*That you may eat the flesh of kings, and the flesh of captains, and the flesh of mighty men, and the flesh of horses, and of them who sit on them, and the flesh of all men, both free and bond, both small and great.* (This proclaims the fact that the Power of Almighty God doesn't blink at those on this Earth who consider themselves to be *'great.'* The Judgment will be identical for all [Ezek. 39:18-20].)

"*And I saw the beast* (John saw the Antichrist leading this mighty army; this is the *'man of sin'* mentioned by Paul in II Thess. Chpt. 2), *and the kings of the Earth, and their armies* (refers to all the Antichrist could get to join him; it includes the *'kings of the East'* of Rev. 16:12), *gathered together to make war against Him Who sat on the horse, and against His army* (refers to Christ and the great army of Heaven, which is with Him; as stated, this is the Battle of Armageddon [Ezek., Chpts. 38-39]).

"*And the beast was taken, and with him the False Prophet who wrought miracles before him* (refers to both of them falling in the Battle of Armageddon), *with which he deceived them who had received the mark of the beast, and them who worshipped his image* (pertains to Satan's chief weapon, which is deception). *These both were cast alive into a lake of fire burning with brimstone* (thus, is the destiny of the Antichrist and the False Prophet, and all who follow them).

"*And the remnant were slain with the sword of Him Who sat upon the horse, which sword proceeded out of His Mouth*

60 *The United States, Israel & Islam*

(the Lord Jesus will speak the word in the Battle of Armageddon, and whatsoever He speaks will take place): *and all the fowls were filled with their flesh.* (This proclaims the end of this conflict. The Antichrist and his hoards will announce to the world what they are going to do regarding Israel, but the end result will be buzzards gorging on their flesh)" (Rev. 19:11-21).

THE MANNER OF THE LORD IN THIS
GREAT VICTORY AT ARMAGEDDON

As is obvious, the Lord will hear the prayer of Israel, will accept that plea and petition, and will come back to rescue His Own, and to take possession of this Earth. In other words, as it regards Satan who at that time will be cast into the bottomless pit, and the Antichrist and all who followed him, they will be cast into Hell (Rev. 19:20; 20:1-3), one might say there is a new sheriff in town, and things are going to be different.

The Lord will unleash the artillery of Heaven against the Antichrist and his vast army, which will include meteorites and blocks of hail, with these blocks, no doubt, weighing a hundred pounds or more. Hundreds of thousands of these *"artillery shells"* and possibly even millions coming from the heavens, the Antichrist doesn't stand a chance. The Scripture says:

"And I will plead against him with pestilence and with blood; and I will rain upon him, and upon his bands, and upon the many people who are with him, an overflowing rain, and great hailstones, fire, and brimstones. (This Verse proclaims the fact that the Lord will use the elements, over which neither the Antichrist nor any other man has any control.)

"Thus will I magnify Myself, and sanctify Myself; and I will be known in the eyes of many nations, they shall know that I am the LORD. (The phrase, 'Thus will I magnify Myself,' has reference to anger held in check for a long time, and then exploding with a fury that defies description)" (Ezek. 38:22-23).

THE TOUCHING DOWN

Christ will come back to the same spot where He left now some 2,000 years ago. Regarding that event, the Angels said:

"You men of Galilee, why do you stand gazing up into Heaven? (This does not mean that it was only men who were present, but rather that this was a common term used for both men and women.) *This same Jesus, which is taken up from*

you into Heaven (refers to the same Human Body with the nail prints in His Hands and Feet, etc.), *so shall come in like manner as you have seen Him go into Heaven* (refers to the same place, which is the Mount of Olivet)" (Acts 1:11).

Concerning the place of His arrival, the Scripture says: *"And His Feet shall stand in that day upon the Mount of Olives, which is before Jerusalem on the east, and the Mount of Olives shall cleave in the midst thereof toward the east and toward the west, and there shall be a very great valley; and half of the mountain shall remove toward the north, and half of it toward the south.* (The first phrase refers to Christ literally standing on the Mount of Olives, which will be His landing point at the Second Coming, fulfilling the prediction of the two Angels at His Ascension [Acts 1:10-11].

"*'And the Mount of Olives shall cleave in the midst thereof toward the east and toward the west,'* actually speaks of a great topographical change, which Israel will use at that hour as a way of escape from the Antichrist. With every road blocked, the Lord will open a way through the very center of the mountain, as He opened a path through the Red Sea.

"*'And there shall be a very great valley,'* refers to the escape route of Israel.

"*'And half of the mountain shall remove toward the north, and half of it toward the south,'* refers to the wall of rock on either side of escaping Israel, which makes it similar to the wall of water on either side when Israel escaped Egypt.)

"*And you shall flee to the valley of the mountains; for the valley of the mountains shall reach unto Azal: yea, you shall flee, like as you fled from before the earthquake in the days of Uzziah king of Judah: and the LORD my God shall come, and all the Saints with you.* (The phrase, '*And you shall flee to the valley of the mountains,*' should read '*through the valley.*' As stated, this will be Israel's escape route from the Antichrist.

"*'For the valley of the mountains shall reach unto Azal,'* probably refers to Beth-ezel, mentioned in Micah 1:11 as a village on the east of Olivet.

"*'Yea, you shall flee,'* is that the people might not be involved in the judgments, which shall fall upon the enemy.

"*'Like as you fled from before the earthquake in the days of Uzziah king of Judah,'* also pertains to an earthquake, which the Lord will use to produce this phenomenon.

"*'And the LORD my God shall come, and all the Saints with you,'* pertains to the Lord coming at this particular time, which

62 *The United States, Israel & Islam*

will have caused the cataclysmic events in the first place. The Passage, *'All the Saints with you,'* refers to every Saint of God who has ever lived being with the Lord at the Second Coming [Rev. 19:14].)

"And it shall come to pass in that day, that the light shall not be clear, nor dark (the phrase, *'And it shall come to pass in that day,'* refers to the very day that Christ appears on Earth, during the Battle of Armageddon. At that time, the day will be extended, thereby giving the Antichrist no respite)*:

"But it shall be one day which shall be known to the LORD, not day, nor night: but it shall come to pass, but at evening time it shall be light. (The entirety of the Battle of Armageddon will last many days; however, the *'day'* mentioned here will probably be extended to last approximately 24 hours)" (Zech. 14:4-7).

THE LORD JESUS CHRIST

When Christ comes back the Second Time, He, and to be sure, will not come back to be beaten, spit upon, caricatured, and crucified, but He will rather come back *"King of kings and Lord of lords."* In other words, whatever needs to be done, He will have the Might and the Power to do it, and to do it instantly.

Israel will know that He is their Messiah, and will, as well, accept Him as Saviour and Lord, and do so immediately. In fact, there will be no doubt as to Who He is. People will not have to ask, *"Is this really the One?"* He will come back with such Power, such Glory, such Magnificence, as to defy all description and, in fact, via Television, the majority of the world will witness His Coming. Concerning this, the Scripture says:

"Behold, He comes with clouds (the Second Coming of Christ is the chief theme of the Book of Revelation; the word *'clouds'* represents great numbers of Saints, i.e., *'clouds of Saints'*); *and every eye shall see Him* (refers to all who will be in the immediate vicinity of Jerusalem, and possibly even billions who may very well see Him by Television), *and they also which pierced Him* (the Jews, and they will then know beyond the shadow of a doubt that Jesus is Messiah and Lord)*: and all kindreds of the earth shall wail because of Him. Even so, Amen.* (The *'wailing'* will take place because of the Judgment Christ will bring upon the world for its sin and shame.)

"I am Alpha and Omega, the beginning and the ending (the First, the Last, the only God), *saith the Lord, which is, and which was, and which is to come, the Almighty.* (The word

'Almighty' guarantees He will be able to accomplish all that He says)" (Rev. 1:7-8).

THE JEWS AND THE LORD JESUS CHRIST

Immediately after His Coming, the Jews will know that He is most definitely their Messiah, but yet at the beginning, they will really not recognize Him as the One they Crucified, i.e., *"the Lord Jesus Christ."*

Concerning that moment, the Scripture says: *"And one shall say unto Him, what are these wounds in your hands? Then He shall answer, those with which I was wounded in the house of My friends.* (In these Passages, the false prophets are placed beside the True Prophet, the Lord Jesus Christ. They, before the Coming of the Lord, too oftentimes were rewarded, while He, as each True Prophet, was greatly opposed, even crucified. The false prophets thrust themselves forward and claim reverence and position; He Himself, the greatest of the Prophets, did not claim to be a professional Prophet — that was not His Mission in coming to Earth — but became a Bond-servant and a Shepherd; made and appointed such in the Divine Purpose of Redemption. For man having sold himself into slavery, it was necessary that Christ should take that position in order to redeem him.

"'And one shall say unto Him,' refers to the moment of recognition, as outlined in Zechariah 12:10, where it says, *'And they shall look upon Me Whom they have pierced, and they shall mourn for Him.'* (This will be shortly after the Second Coming, with the Antichrist now defeated and Christ standing before Israel. They will then know, and beyond the shadow of a doubt, that He is the Messiah; then they will ask, *'What are these wounds in Your Hands?'*

"These wounds, which He will ever carry, will be an instant and constant reminder of Who He is and what was done to Him, which presents Him as the Sin-Bearer of the world. Even though He was the Redeemer of all mankind, still, this shows how He was treated by man, especially by His Own.

"'Then He shall answer,' will be an answer that will cause their terrible *'mourning'* of Zechariah 12:10-14. It will also be the cause of the *'Fountain opened to the House of David and to the inhabitants of Jerusalem for sin and for uncleanness.'*

"'Those with which I was wounded in the house of My friends' proclaims His Crucifixion and those who did it to Him. The words, *'My friends,'* are said in irony.)

64 *The United States, Israel & Islam*

"*Awake, O sword, against My Shepherd, and against the Man Who is My Fellow, saith the LORD of Hosts: smite the Shepherd, and the sheep shall be scattered: and I will turn My hand upon the little ones.* (The phrase, '*Awake, O sword, against My Shepherd,*' concerns the Crucifixion of Christ, because Christ was the '*Good Shepherd*' [Jn. 10:11], in effect, '*God's Shepherd.*'

"'*And against the Man Who is My Fellow, saith the LORD of Hosts,*' refers to Christ as the '*Fellow*' of Jehovah.

"'*Smite the Shepherd,*' pertains to the fact that not only was sin upon the sinless Substitute at Calvary, but the Substitute Himself, Jehovah's equal. He Himself must die in order that man might live; for the curse that rested upon man was the doom of death [separation from God] because of sin. Christ's Death was, therefore, necessary to satisfy that claim and to vindicate and magnify Divine Righteousness.

"'*And the sheep shall be scattered,*' pertains to them '*scattered*' as a Nation, but not finally lost, for His Hand, pierced by the flock, shall cause the '*little ones*' to return to Zion, which these Passages and many others proclaim!

"'*And I will turn My Hand upon the little ones,*' pertains to the Coming of the Lord and the Restoration of Israel, which will bring '*the little ones*' back.

"In astronomy, a near Planet and a distant fixed star may appear side-by-side in the heavens, though the one is millions of miles more distant than the other; so, in the Scriptures, often two Prophecies may be side-by-side in the Text but, as here, be separated by many hundreds, sometimes thousands of years)" (Zech. 13:6-7).

THE KINGDOM AGE

With the Second Coming, the Kingdom Age will now begin, an Age that will last for 1,000 years. War will then be a thing of the past. The Scripture says:

"*And they shall beat their swords into plowshares, and their spears into pruninghooks: nation shall not lift up sword against nation, neither shall they learn war anymore*" (Isa. 2:4).

The very natures of both man and beast will be changed. The Scripture says:

"*The wolf also shall dwell with the lamb, and the leopard shall lie down with the kid; and the calf and the young lion and the fatling together; and a little child shall lead them.* (The character and nature of the Planet, including its occupants and even the animal creation, will revert to their posture as before the Fall.)

"And the cow and the bear shall feed (feed together); their young ones shall lie down together: and the lion shall eat straw like the ox. (This Passage plainly tells us that the carnivorous nature of the animal kingdom will be totally and eternally changed.)

"And the sucking child shall play on the hole of the asp, and the weaned child shall put his hand on the cockatrice den. (Even though some of the curse will remain on the serpent in the Millennium, in that he continues to writhe in the dust, still, the deadly part will be removed [Gen. 3:14])" (Isa. 11:6-8).

Sickness will be a thing of the past. The Scripture says:

"And the inhabitant shall not say, I am sick: the people who dwell therein shall be forgiven their iniquity. (When sin is abolished, sickness shall no more exist. The one is the cause; the other, the effect. This will be the blessing of the coming Kingdom Age, when Christ will reign Personally and Supreme.)" (Isa. 33:24).

Israel at that time, now washed and cleansed by the Blood of the Lamb, would serve under Christ as the Priestly Nation of the world. Ezekiel described this rule in Chapters 40 through 48 of his great Book.

In Truth, we've only touched a few highlights of what will take place in the coming Kingdom Age. But all of it, the prosperity, the freedom, the joy and happiness which will prevail, will all be because of Christ. He will reign Personally from Jerusalem. In fact, Ezekiel closed his great Book by saying, "The LORD is there."

The phrase, "The LORD is there," means in Hebrew, "Adonai-Shammah" or "Jehovah-Shammah," meaning literally what it says. For the Messiah will be there reigning visibly and eternally in Israel [Isa. 9:6-7; Lk. 1:32-33; Rev. 11:15; 20:4-10])" (Ezek. 48:35).

But we must never forget, all of this, and without exception, has been made possible by the Cross of Christ (Isa., Chpt. 53).

EPILOGUE

Counting all the side issues, it is believed that the 9/11 (September 9, 2001) attack by the Muslims cost this nation one trillion dollars. We've already spent six-hundred billion in Iraq, and that's not included in the trillion just mentioned and, as well, the powers that be, say that if we stay the course in Iraq, whatever that means, it will cost another trillion dollars. So that makes the situation with the Muslims, having already cost one trillion, six-hundred billion, quite possibly, before it's over, costing two trillion, six-hundred billion. That's besides all the blood that was shed on 9/11, and that which has been shed in Iraq.

Every bit of it is because of that religion.

IDEOLOGY

I'm noticing news pundants and commentators beginning to use the word *"ideology,"* as it refers to the Muslim religion. In other words, the few fanatics having hijacked this wonderful religion, seems to be slowly falling by the wayside. The pregnancy, so to speak, is becoming too difficult to hide.

The word *"ideology"* refers to *"a systematic body of concepts about human life or culture."* In their thinking, we've got to change their ideology.

Most do not seem to understand, that it's the religion of Islam that is the problem. It is not a mere ideology. Ideologies can be changed, but religions cannot be changed. We're wasting our time, efforts, money, treasure, and blood, thinking that we can. Have we changed anything in Iraq? As I've already stated in this short volume, our policy is built on a lie. We have taken a position that the religion of Islam is a wonderful, peaceable religion, which has been hijacked by a few fanatics. If we will only show the Muslims how much we want to be friends with them, then they will see the light.

FRIENDS?

The Muslims are buying into our Media companies, which in

some cases gives them enough sway that they can somewhat control what is being said over the news media. For instance, when thousands of automobiles were being burned in France by Muslims some time ago, and we were reporting it here in the States thusly, I'm told that Rupert Murdock was called by a Muslim prince who had invested many millions of dollars in Fox News, requesting that the perpetrators of the burning of the automobiles in France not be referred to as Muslims, but rather "*underprivileged young people.*" I'm told that Murdock acquiesced, with the verbiage instantly being changed.

Our Schools and our Universities are, as well, being invaded. The Muslims begin first of all, and we refer to those who are very rich with oil money, giving millions of dollars to respective Universities. In this fashion, they can have a voice in what is taught in these Universities, with, to be certain, nothing derogatory said about the religion of Islam. In other words, they are taking the money we use to buy their oil, sending it back to us, at least a small portion, attempting to influence elections, the curriculum of Schools and Universities, etc. and they are succeeding all too well.

As an aside, if the tree-huggers would allow us to drill for oil in Alaska, and as well many other places in the U.S.A. known to have reserves of oil, we could cut our dependence for Saudi oil at least by half. The great reservoirs of oil go untapped in this country, and almost all of the time, for very foolish reasons. The upshot is, the Muslims aren't our friends. In countries ruled by Islam, when the little children enter school, they are taught from Kindergarten to hate Americans and to hate Israelis. They are fed a steady diet of venom all the days of their life, which makes many of them perfectly willing to be human bombers when the time comes. As I've already stated, we are facing something our nation has never faced before, and we're conducting ourselves very unwisely.

MODERATES?

Are there moderate Muslims who do not desire to kill, to mutilate, etc.?

Yes, there are.

In fact, we are told that only about 10 percent of the Muslims fall into the category of "*fanatics;*" however, we should keep it in mind, that there are about a billion Muslims in the world, and 10 percent of a billion is 100 million. So, we have an awful lot of fanatics out there hungering for the blood of the "*infidel,*" as they put it. But what about the overwhelming majority of

68 *The United States, Israel & Islam*

approximately 900 million?

The truth is, a large percentage of that 900 million, although not murderers themselves, still, are in sympathy with the rabid percentage. They don't say anything, but in their heart of hearts, they are in perfect sympathy with what is taking place. In fact, many of those who serve as the leaders of respective Muslim countries, while claiming to be our friends, are secretly working, and sometimes not so secretly, to aid and abet those who are doing the dirty work.

And then there is a percentage of Muslims who are not murderers, and who possibly are not in sympathy with those who do fall into that ghastly category. So, the question is asked as to why these Muslims, ever how many there might be of them, don't make themselves heard as it regards their opposition to the barbarism that's taking place in the Muslim world?

There is an excellent reason as to why they aren't vocal in their opposition, if, in fact, they are opposed! They too will quickly be put on the hit list. In other words, if they speak out against the terrorism that's taking place in their religion, their voices will be silenced very quickly, and in brutal fashion.

Above all, they know this, so they elect to say nothing.

So, if we think that these *"moderates"* are going to gradually gain the upper hand and eventually stop the murder and the barbarism, we had better think again. It's not going to happen! As we've previously stated, religions do not change, except for the worse. Politicians who have it in their minds that this evil can be ameliorated, can be soothed and changed for the better, at the very first opportunity, we had better turn these individuals out of office. But the problem is, sadly and regrettably, almost all of our politicians fall into this category. If there is a lone voice somewhere that does speak the truth, and I'm referring to the political realm, he is soon shouted down, as being intolerant and thus, spewing out hate.

In England they have already come to the place in their government, that the word *"Muslim"* is not to be linked with terrorism, but always is to be spoken of in a good sense. How far behind our English cousins are we in instituting the same ridiculous policy? I'm afraid that Uncle Sam is quickly being replaced with Uncle Sap!

CHRISTIANS

As Believers in the Lord Jesus Christ, we must pray for the

Muslims. Their darkness is painful and eternal. There is no hope for them, as there is no hope for anyone, other than the Lord Jesus Christ. As it regards any Muslims with whom we possibly might have contact, as Believers, we will treat them kindly and with respect; however, we will do so with the understanding as to what they really are.

In Truth, Believers can do more to address this terrible situation, by seeking the Face of the Lord than anyone else and anything else. Prayer still works wonders, still brings about miracles, still is the answer. We should, as well, pray for our leaders and do so on a daily basis, that somehow the Wisdom of God will come to them, that the decisions they make, might be the right decisions. In fact, we are importuned in the Word of God to do exactly that. The Scripture says:

"*I exhort therefore* (resumes and develops Paul's charge to Timothy, which began in I Tim. 1:18), *that, first of all* (it is as if Paul said, '*the most important point in this exhortation concerns the universal scope of prayer*'), *supplications* (personal needs), *prayers* (petitions), *intercessions* (in this case, an approach to God on the basis of an accepted relationship), *and giving of thanks* (Praise and Worship), *be made for all men* (lends credence to the idea that we should pray about everything);

"*For kings, and for all who are in authority* (Civil government); *that we may lead a quiet and peaceable life in all Godliness and honesty.* (This speaks of Government that's free of turmoil, about which prayer can have a great affect.)

"*For this is good and acceptable in the sight of God our Saviour* (refers to this being the Will of God and for all the obvious reasons);

"*Who will have all men to be Saved* (presents Salvation, which is universal in virtue and aim), *and to come unto the knowledge of the Truth.* (This pertains to Salvation through Jesus Christ and what He did at the Cross [Jn. 3:16; Rom. 6:3-6; 10:9-10])" (I Tim. 2:1-4).

Christians must know and understand, there can be no agreement with the religion of Islam. While we love these people, and we should show our love, still, the religion of Islam is not of God, but rather of the Evil One. We do not do Muslims a favor by making them think that we think they are Saved. Sadly and regrettably, they aren't! The Scripture says:

"*And what concord has Christ with Belial?* (This presents another name for Satan.) *Or what part has he who believes with an infidel?*

70 *The United States, Israel & Islam*

"And what agreement has the Temple of God with idols? For you are the Temple of the Living God (speaking of all Believers); *as God has said* (Ex. 29:45; Lev. 26:12; Ezek. 37:27), *I will dwell in them, and walk in them; and I will be their God, and they shall be My people"* (II Cor. 6:15-16).

WHAT CHRISTIANS SHOULD KNOW ABOUT IRAQ

While the Bible says nothing about the religion of Islam, at least directly, it has much to say about the country of Iraq, known in Bible times as Mesopotamia, the Assyrian Empire, Babylon, or the Chaldees.

Please note the following:

• It is believed by some Bible Scholars that the Garden of Eden was situated where ancient Babylon was later built, which is in Iraq. It is a fact that *"A river went out of Eden to water the Garden; and from thence it was parted, and became into four heads"* (Gen. 2:10). Of those four rivers one is named *"Hiddekel,"* which is believed to be the Tigris, and the other one is the *"Euphrates"* (Gen. 2:14).

• Man was created in Iraq, and then placed in the Garden of Eden (Gen. 2:7-8).

• *"The Tree of Life,"* and the *"Tree of Knowledge of Good and Evil"* were located in the Garden of Eden, i.e., *"Iraq."*

• The Lord, in the country of Iraq taught man Agriculture and Agronomy (Gen. 2:15).

• The first prohibition regarding evil was given by God to Adam and Eve in Iraq (Gen. 2:16-17).

• All of the animals were created by God in Iraq (Gen. 2:19-20).

• The Lord created woman in Iraq (Gen. 2:21-22).

• The first marriage was performed in Iraq, which was the act of God performing the ceremony as it regards Adam and Eve (Gen. 2:23-24).

• The first temptation instituted by Satan using the serpent, seeking to induce Adam and Eve to partake of the forbidden fruit, was in Iraq (Gen. 3:1-5).

• The first sin was committed in Iraq when Eve first of all ate the forbidden fruit followed by her husband Adam (Gen. 3:6).

• The *"Fall"* took place in Iraq, when both Adam and Eve fell from the high position of total God-consciousness, down to the far, far lower level of total self-consciousness, which ushered in all the evil that now plagues the world (Gen. 3:7-13).

• Because of sin, the first curse was leveled at the serpent

Epilogue **71**

for allowing himself to be used by Satan (Gen. 3:14). It was done in Iraq.

• The first Prophecy was given by the Lord in Iraq, and it concerned the coming of the Redeemer, the Lord Jesus Christ, and the price He would pay on Calvary's Cross in order that man might be redeemed (Gen. 3:15).

• In Iraq the sorrow of woman was multiplied as it regards conception, i.e., the bringing of children into the world in sorrow instead of gladness (Gen. 3:16).

• In Iraq, and because of her failure, woman was reduced to less than originally created, by her husband now having rule over her (Gen. 3:16).

• In Iraq the very ground of the earth was cursed, and because of Adam's sin, which has greatly curtailed the production of foodstuff from then until now (Gen. 3:17-18).

• In Iraq the sentence of death was passed upon all of mankind, and because of sin (Gen. 3:19).

• In Iraq the first symbolism of Redemption was carried out by the Lord *"making coats of skins and clothing Adam and Eve,"* which took the place of their fig leaves. Animals had to die for these coats of skins to be afforded, which symbolized what Christ would do in order to cover the sin of man, which was carried out at Calvary's Cross (Gen. 3:21).

• It was in Iraq that the first Sacrifice of sin was offered up by Abel, and was accepted by the Lord (Gen. 4:4).

• It was in Iraq that the first bloodless sacrifice was offered up, and done so by Cain, the brother of Abel. It was not accepted by the Lord. Regrettably, the offering up of such sacrifices has continued from then until now (Gen. 4:3-5).

• The first murder was committed in Iraq, as Cain murdered his brother in cold blood, because he was angry that God accepted the Sacrifice of his brother, which was the sacrifice of an innocent victim, a lamb, and would not accept his offering of vegetables or fruit (Gen. 4:8).

• It is believed that it was in Iraq that Noah built the Ark (Gen. 6:14).

• It is believed that it was in Iraq that the flood began, which shortly was to cover the entirety of the Earth, in which it destroyed all things, with the exception of Noah, his family, and all that were in the Ark (Gen. 6:17).

• The Tower of Babel was constructed in Iraq, which was the first organized rebellion against God (Gen. 11:4).

• It was in Iraq that the language of men, which had been

72 *The United States, Israel & Islam*

one language previously, was now multiplied by God into many (Gen. 11:6-7).

• It was in Iraq, Ur of the Chaldees where God revealed Himself to Abraham (Gen. 11:31; 12:1).

• It was in Iraq that the Lord gave to Abraham the great promise, *"And I will make of you a great Nation, and I will bless you, and make your name great; and you shall be a blessing: and I will bless them who bless you, and curse him who curses you: and in you shall all the families of the earth be Blessed"* (Gen. 12:2-3).

• It was the Assyrian Empire, which was in the boundaries of modern day Iraq, that destroyed the northern kingdom of Israel, which God allowed to happen, and because of Israel's great sin (II Ki. 17:5-23).

• It was against the Assyrian king Sennacherib, who had invaded the southern Kingdom of Judah, against which the Lord sent one Angel, and 185,000 Assyrians died in one night (II Ki. 18:13, 34-35).

• It was the Babylonian Empire, which was allowed by God as well to destroy Judah and Jerusalem, and because of Judah's great sin (II Ki. 25:8-10), which empire was in Iraq.

• It was in Iraq, i.e., *"Babylon,"* that the Children of Israel spent some 70 years in captivity, and because of their great sin (II Chron. 36:20).

• It was in Iraq that Nebuchadnezzar the king had a dream, in which he saw the future kingdoms of the world, which dream was interpreted by Daniel (Dan. 2:1, 19).

• It was in Iraq that the image of gold was constructed, and that all had to worship it. The three Hebrew children refused, with God performing a mighty Miracle in the fiery furnace, and saving their lives (Dan. 3:1, 5-6, 11, 23, 25).

• It was in Babylon that Daniel had his dreams and visions, which again portrayed the future kingdoms of the world, which would persecute Israel (Dan., Chpts. 7-12).

• It was from Iraq, i.e., *"Babylon,"* that Daniel wrote the Book in the Bible that bears his name, which is the most comprehensive description of coming World Empires, and Endtime events, found in the Bible, or anywhere for that matter.

• It was to Nineveh in Iraq, that Jonah the Prophet was called of God to go and preach against their wickedness. This was the first city outside of Israel to have such a privilege. Nineveh repented.

• The short book of Nahum in the Old Testament presents

Epilogue **73**

this Prophet predicting the fall of that city, which took place in 612 B.C. This was about 150 years after Jonah had ministered there. Regrettably, whereas Nineveh repented under the preaching of Jonah, they ignored the great prediction given by God through Nahum, and went to their doom.

• Both Epistles in the New Testament of Peter the Apostle were written from Babylon, which is in Iraq (I Pet. 5:13).

• The great whore of Revelation 17:1 is described as *"MYSTERY, BABYLON THE GREAT, THE MOTHER OF HARLOTS AND ABOMINATIONS OF THE EARTH."* This is symbolic of all the religions that have ever existed, with religion being that which is devised totally by man and not at all by God (Rev. 17:1-5).

• Revelation, Chapter 18 portrays literal Babylon or the spirit of Babylon being utterly destroyed, which will take place immediately before the Second Coming. In truth, the city of Babylon is mentioned more times in the Bible than any other city, with the exception of Jerusalem. The former portrays the effort of the Evil One to steal, kill, and destroy, with the latter portraying that which is of God. In other words, both cities, Babylon and Jerusalem, stand in contrast. That contrast has existed, as stated, almost from the time of the flood unto the present. It will not end until the Second Coming. In fact, it is believed that the Antichrist will make his first headquarters in rebuilt Babylon, or could it be Dubai?

One thing is certain, Babylon, or the Babylonian spirit, will play a great part in Endtime events, which, in effect, have already begun to come to pass.

> *"I will sing the wondrous Story,*
> *"Of the Christ Who died for me,*
> *"How He left His Home in Glory,*
> *"For the Cross on Calvary."*
>
> *"I was lost, but Jesus found me,*
> *"Found the sheep that was astray;*
> *"Threw His loving Arms around me,*
> *"Drew me back into His Way."*
>
> *"I was bruised, but Jesus healed me,*
> *"Faint was I from many a fall,*
> *"Sight was gone, and fears possessed me,*
> *"But He freed me from them all."*

74 *The United States, Israel & Islam*

*"Days of darkness still come o'er me,
"Sorrow's paths how often tread,
"But the Saviour still is with me,
"By His Hand I'm safely led."*

*"He will keep me till the river,
"Rolls its waters at my feet;
"Then He'll bear me safely over,
"Where the loved ones I shall meet."*